JUXTASIX

Research and Scholarship in Haiku

2020

THE *Haiku* FOUNDATION

JUXTASIX

ISBN 978-0-9826951-7-3
Copyright © 2020 by The Haiku Foundation

JUXTASIX is the print version of *Juxtapositions* 6.1.
A journal of haiku research and scholarship,
Juxtapositions is published by The Haiku Foundation.

The Haiku Foundation
PO Box 2461
Winchester VA
22604-1661 USA
www.thehaikufoundation.org/juxta

Contents

Editor's Welcome

Stepping into the role of Senior Editor, I want to express my appreciation to Peter McDonald for his fine work overseeing five issues of *Juxtapositions*. Without his leadership as Senior Editor, the journal would not have had such a solid start and we would not be in the position to continue with *Juxtapositions* 6.

Our editorial board has undergone additional changes in the past year. Randy M. Brooks and Bill Cooper have stepped down, and I want to extend great thanks for their insights and contributions from the beginning of this journal in 2014 to its current iteration. We have several people joining us, as well. Welcome to the new members of our editorial board: Josh Hockensmith, Adam Kern, and Crystal Simone Smith. Welcome, also, to our new Book Review Editor, David Grayson. Their energy and ideas are already guiding us toward an exciting *Juxtapositions* 7 in 2021.

In this sixth issue, readers will find the continuation of an inquiry into the relationship between eye movement and cognition, and the role that haiku is playing in discovering that relationship, that began with "Haiku and the Brain" in *Juxta* 3, and continued with "Knocking on the Doors of Perception" in *Juxta* 5; an examination of the arrangement of Richard Wright's haiku; and a consideration of Etheridge Knight's haiku including the first-time publication of several haiku from the Knight archives. Reviews of *Jack Kerouac and the Traditions of Classic and Modern Haiku* and *Haiku in Canada: History, Poetry, Memoir*, as well as a selection of fine haiga, round out *Juxta* 6. Thank you to all of our contributors.

Finally, I would like to thank Jim Kacian and The Haiku Foundation for publishing what continues to be the only peer-reviewed journal of haiku scholarship in English.

On behalf of all the editors who worked on this issue, please enjoy *Juxtapositions* 6.

Ce Rosenow
Senior Editor

daymoon
gossamery
in the blue

Poet: an'ya
Artist: Ed Baker

Reading haiku:

Semantic distance and the 'cut effect'

Thomas Geyer[1], Quirin Würschinger[2],
Jim Kacian[3], Heinrich R. Liesefeld[1],
Hermann J. Müller[1] & Stella Pierides[3]

ABSTRACT: In our previous studies, we monitored readers' eye movements while they were reading normative 3-line English-language haiku, consisting of two images – a fragment (1 line) and a phrase (2 lines) – separated by a cut. We found that, in their attempt to understand the haiku, our readers' eyes dwelled longer on words in the fragment line compared to the phrase lines, and this 'cut effect' was more marked for 'juxtaposition' haiku than for 'context–action' haiku. We proposed that meaning resolution is concentrated on the fragment line and that fusing the juxtaposed images is the harder the farther apart they are conceptually. To test this, drawing on novel techniques from computational linguistics, we used a neural network language model to determine the 'semantic similarity' between fragment and phrase for each haiku in our sample. We then assessed whether this measure would predict the observed eye-movement patterns. While we found semantic similarity to influence the cut effect, the relationship was actually opposite to the prediction for context–action haiku, and similarity was not higher for juxtaposition haiku. We discuss possible reasons for these findings and why extant measures of conceptual-semantic similarity might be limited in explaining the cut effect.

1. General and Experimental Psychology, LMU, Munich, Germany.
2. Department of English and American Studies, LMU, Munich, Germany.
3. The Haiku Foundation, Winchester, VA, USA.

Semantic Distance and the 'Cut Effect'

Haiku poets, and scientists in the field of Neurocognitive Poetics alike, have wondered what it is that contributes to the insight, the sudden understanding of haiku, the 'aha moment' that a reader experiences while reading a well-written poem. To approach this question, we began by examining how readers of normative 3-line English-language haiku read this form of poetry—which typically consists of two image elements: 'fragment' and 'phrase', that are separated by a conceptual 'gap' or 'cut' and thus require the reader to invest mental effort to align the images (i.e., construct a bridging context) and achieve an understanding of the haiku. Specifically, by examining readers' eye movements while they scanned and re-scanned the poems' lines, we were able to gain some insight into how attentive reading, assessed by means of eye movements, contributes to the integration of the (seemingly) discrepant fragment and phrase elements. The key findings were as follows (a comprehensive report of the results can be found in Geyer et al.; see also Pierides et al.):

The eyes, and thus the mind, spend more time (per word) in the poem's fragment line compared to the phrase lines – a finding we referred to as 'cut effect'.[1] For instance, in "bruised apples / he wonders what else / I haven't told him" (M. Allen), the reading time (per word) is longest in the fragment line "bruised apples". This is true whether the cut occurs at the end of line 1 (like in the above example) or at the end of line 2 ("closing my eyes / to find it / cricket's song"; B. Antonio), and whether the poem is, in Kacian's (*How to Haiku*) terminology, classed as a 'context–action haiku' ("closing my eyes …") or a 'juxtaposition' haiku ("bruised apples …"). In contrast, no such pattern is evident in uncut, one-image haiku, in which the eyes dwell for similar amounts

1. Technically, the cut effect is the additional time the eyes spent per word in the poem's fragment compared to the remote phrase line, i.e., line 1 in haiku with a cut after line 2 or line 3 in haiku with a cut after line 1.

of time (per word) in all lines. Thus, the cut effect in two-image haiku indicates that much of the mental work to integrate the two images into a coherent 'reading' is concentrated on the fragment line. That is, the reader treats the fragment as being pivotal for global meaning construction: it is, ultimately, in the fragment line that the tension between the two images is resolved.

Furthermore, while we observed a cut in both context–action and juxtaposition haiku, the type of poem made a difference: our readers spent relatively more time (per word) in the fragment line, compared to the phrase lines, in juxtaposition haiku (e.g., on "bruised apples") than in context–action haiku (e.g., on "cricket's song"). We attributed this to the strength of the juxtaposition varying between the two types of haiku. In context–action haiku, one of the images clearly establishes the setting where the haiku moment is experienced; the other suggests the activity which caught the notice of the poet's imagination. So, for the reader, the gap between the two images is more straightforward to close. In juxtaposition haiku, by contrast, two images not obviously related by context or action are paired, making it more difficult to bridge the gap between the two disparate parts.

Effective reading and achieving an understanding of a given haiku may thus be a function of the availability or 'constructability' of a cognitive model, or cut-resolution schema (e.g., based on acquired context–action associations). Accordingly, a straightforward hypothesis would be that the cut effect is a function of cognitive-linguistic properties of individual haiku, in particular, how close vs. how distant the images evoked in the fragment and phrase lines are in semantic space, that is: the cut effect is the larger the further apart the images are. This would potentially also explain why the cut effect is overall smaller for context–action haiku: as an instantiation of the basic figure–ground schema (Langacker; Talmy, "Fictive motion in language and 'caption'"; Talmy, "Toward a Cognitive Semantics"), 'context–action' is the most fundamental, and thus the most readily available, general type of mental schema we have to construct 'episodic' representations. That is, as a result of experience from early childhood on, certain actions become intrinsically linked with certain contexts, so that the action becomes predictable, or is 'primed', by invoking the context. As a result, due to the ready availability of linking schemata, the semantic distance between fragment (context image) and phrase (action image) would be smaller for context–action vs. juxtaposition haiku, making it easier to bridge the conceptual gap between the juxtaposed images. In fact, when we submitted our original articles for review in scientific journals, (some) reviewers considered the finding of a larger cut effect for juxtaposition haiku 'trivial', because they deemed it to simply reflect the greater semantic distance between fragment and phrase compared to context–action haiku.

This raises a fundamental question: can the cut effect simply be reduced to an effect of semantic distance — or its flipside: semantic similarity — between fragment and phrase? And, related to this, does semantic distance have similar effects in context–action and juxtaposition haiku (as would be predicted on the semantic-distance hypothesis)?

In order to address these issues in a way that avoids circular reasoning, one needs to have an independent measure of the semantic distance between fragment and phrase. To obtain such a measure, we made use of recent advances in language modeling using machine learning. Most advances in Natural Language Processing[2] in recent years have

---

2. Liddy, in the *Encyclopedia of Library and Information Science*, defines "Natural Language Processing … [as] a theoretically motivated range of computational techniques for analyzing and representing naturally occurring texts at one or more levels of linguistic analysis for the purpose of achieving human-like language processing for a range of tasks or applications".

been driven by so-called 'deep learning' models: artificial neural networks composed of several layers of interconnected 'neural' units—with one or more 'hidden' layers between the input and output units. In the linguistic domain, these models form the distributional semantic representations of words by systematically learning their co-occurrence pattern from large collections of textual data. According to distributional-semantic theory—"You shall know a word by the company it keeps" (Firth 11)—words that co-occur are more likely to be semantically similar. State-of-the-art models such as 'BERT' (see below for details) are trained to predict 'masked' words and sentences in the input, which allows them to learn contextual semantic representations of individual words and larger units of text. While the architecture and learning processes of current artificial neural networks can hardly be compared to human language learning, some basic principles are shared: algorithms like BERT learn to form semantic representations of linguistic constituents by drawing on distributional patterns in large amounts of linguistic input (thus approximating human experience with language).[3]

---

3. That is, during training, words and sentences in the input are masked to the neural language model and the network is made to guess, or 'predict', what the masked items are (as the output). Prediction errors (on the output layer) are fed, or 'propagated', back through the network (from the output to the input layer) to adjust, or 'tune', the strengths of the connections between neural units so as to reduce the prediction error. As a result of continual refinement of neural connections over the course of training (during which the network is exposed to large language corpora), the network becomes increasingly better in predicting the missing items. In some sense, this is similar to human language acquisition: the neural language model learns from experience to extract and represent, in its internal connectivity structure, the concepts and their interrelations inherent in the linguistic input. Based on these semantic representations, the network becomes able to 'fill in' adequate items from partial input, such as missing words in a sentence.

A core feature of the vector[4] representation format (i.e., capturing the semantic content of words as numerical feature vectors in a shared, high-dimensional Euclidean space) is that it allows semantic similarity of linguistic constituents to be measured quantitatively. Commonly, cosine similarity between vectors is used to assess the degree of similarity between two linguistic units. The cosine similarity of two vectors ranges between 0 and 1: it is 1 if two vectors are parallel, and 0 if they are orthogonal. Thus, higher values indicate greater semantic similarity, lower values greater semantic distance.

The particular model we made use of for our purposes is Google's model named BERT (short for 'Bidirectional Encoder Representations from Transformers'; Devlin, Chang, Lee, & Toutanova), whose transformer architecture has recently produced significant advances in many domains of natural language processing. BERT's language model was trained on more than three billion words of text from Wikipedia and BookCorpus. Most importantly for the present research context, transfer learning makes it possible to use the model's pre-trained representations and apply them to data-sparse domains like the present one, which would be too small to train a language model from scratch. Besides, BERT's contextual representations allow for more nuanced semantic analyses, which are particularly important for analyzing poetic language. Thus, by combining vector-space information for

---

4. A vector is a mathematical 'object' that has both a magnitude and a direction. Geometrically, a vector can be depicted as a directed line segment, with the length of the segment corresponding to its magnitude and with an arrowhead indicating its direction. A simple example in two-dimensional (Euclidian) space would be the direction and distance one would have to travel to reach a certain destination from a given starting point: neither the direction alone nor the distance alone would be sufficient to specify how to get to the destination. The cosine of the angle between two vectors in n-dimensional (i.e., two- and higher-dimensional) space provides a measure of the similarity between them.

individual tokens, we can model the semantic content of spans of text of variable size. This enables us to calculate the semantic distance between single lines as well as between fragment and phrase of a haiku.

Applied to the poems we presented to our readers in Geyer et al., BERT enabled us to compute the semantic similarity between individual haiku's fragment and phrase lines, essentially determining how near or far apart in semantic space the 'contents' in the fragment and phrase lines are. We then used these semantic similarity measures to retrospectively 'predict' the cut effect (taken to be indicative of the meaning resolution processes) that a given haiku gave rise to.

To understand the main results of this explorative analysis (which we sketch below), it is useful to recapitulate some of the key methodological details of the eye-movement study of Geyer et al. In this study, we tested 21 native English-language speakers (who were 'naïve' with regard to the genre of haiku) during the reading of 64 two-image haiku, with a clearly discernible cut either after line 1 or after line 2. One of the main experimental manipulations was the type of poems: 32 of the haiku were of the context–action type, and 32 of the juxtaposition variety. Of note, our readers were asked to read the poems for their understanding and were given sufficient time to read a given haiku several times before moving on to the next poem.

While they read each of the poems, we recorded our participants' eye movements and fixations using a remote eye-tracker device. Technically, a fixation is the period during which the eye stands still between two movements, and it is (only) during fixations that visual information is taken up by the eye. Reading eye-movement research is predicated on the so-called 'eye-mind-assumption' (Just & Carpenter): eye movements tell us where, when, and for how long attention is allocated within the text to extract information and integrate it into global meaning. Thus, based on our readers eye-movement record, we could discern for how long they fixated each word in the fragment and phrase lines of a given poem. While the general scanning direction is from left to right and top to bottom, the reading of haiku is characterized by highly complex eye-movement patterns: readers move forward and backward within each poem line and may re-read parts or the whole of the poem several times. Thus, to reduce this complexity and quantify the cut effect, we determined the so-called 'dwell' time (i.e., the sum of fixation durations) per word in the fragment line and subtracted from this the dwell time per word in the 'remote' phrase line (i.e., line 3 in haiku with a cut at the end of line 2 and line 1 in haiku with a cut at the end of line 1). We used 'remote' phrase line for comparison because, in normative three-line haiku, this line is most comparable in length to the fragment line (in addition, the fragment and phrase lines were equated in terms of word length and word frequency, amongst other linguistic factors that could influence fixation durations). The results are essentially unchanged if we take the second line into account (see Müller et al. and Geyer et al. for details).

To determine a relationship between the eye-movement patterns obtained by Geyer et al. and semantic similarity, we performed correlation analysis between the cut effect — the additional time the eyes spent per word in the poem's fragment compared to the phrase lines — and the measure of semantic 'similarity' (or, its flipside: semantic 'distance') computed by the language model.

As a preliminary analysis, we examined whether the semantic similarity measures returned by BERT characterizes 'meaningful' linguistic units in our sample haiku. In particular, the semantic similarity should be higher between the two phrase lines of a given poem (which together form one image) than between the fragment line and the phrase lines (which form separate images). Our preliminary analysis confirmed this to be the case. Accordingly, being reassured that our method to quantify semantic similarity is valid, we proceeded to examine the relationship between the (model-derived) semantic similarity estimates and the cut effects (quantified in milliseconds extra reading time per word, with the cut effect averaged across the 21 participants in the study of Geyer et al.), separately for context–action and juxtaposition haiku.

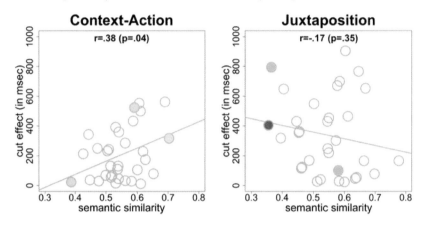

Figure 1: Relationship between the cut effect and semantic similarity, separately for context–action and juxtaposition haiku (see text for explanations).

The results of this correlation analysis are presented in Figure 1. The x-axis of the figure represents the semantic similarity between the fragment and phrase lines, as derived from BERT (cosine similarity values ranging from 0 to 1), and the y-axis the observed cut effect measured in milliseconds (msec) extra reading time per word (values ranging from 0 to 1000 msec). Each circle in the two panels (context–action haiku on the left and juxtaposition haiku on the right) represents one particular poem. For instance, for the context–action haiku marked by the filled yellow circle, the semantic-similarity score computed by BERT was about .70 and the observed cut effect (averaged across the 21 readers who took part in the study of Geyer et al.) was about 300 msec; and for the juxtaposition haiku marked by the filled red circle, the semantic similarity was about .35 and the cut effect 400 msec. As can be seen, the individual data points in the two panels show a good deal of scatter, forming more or less dense 'clouds'. To discern a relationship in this scatter, in correlation analysis, a linear function is fitted to the cloud such that the data points' deviation from the line is minimal. The resulting (so-called 'regression') lines — which encapsulate the relationship between the cut effect and semantic similarity — are depicted in the two panels of Figure 1.[5]

As can be seen from Figure 1, the results of this analysis turned out somewhat surprising and, at first sight, counter-intuitive. For context–action haiku, there is a significant positive relationship (indicated by the regression line ascending from the left to the right): $r = .38$, $p = .04$; that is, the cut effect is the greater the higher the semantic similarity between a poem's fragment and phrase. This runs counter to the expected negative correlation, that is: the cut effect should decrease with increasing semantic similarity (as the semantic-conceptual gap between the two juxtaposed images gets smaller). Also of note, although the correlation is significant and so does have explanatory value, it accounts for only some 15% of the variance in the cut effect .[6]

In contrast, for juxtaposition haiku, there appears to be a slightly negative trend of the cut effect decreasing with increasing similarity

5. Statistically, the degree of the association is quantified by the correlation coefficient r, which can range between 0 (no relationship) and 1 (perfect relationship). The closer the data points cluster around the line, the higher, and the more reliable, the correlation (for a perfect correlation, all data points would have to lie exactly on the line). The probability value p associated with the correlation coefficient r gives the likelihood of the observed correlation if the true correlation in the population is zero (i.e., a flat function), which should be less than 5% (the standard criterion of significance) for the observed correlation to be considered significant (i.e., $p < .05$).

6. The effective effect size of the correlation coefficient r is r2, i.e., in our case: $0.382 = .14$.

(the regression line descends from the left to the right), which was however not statistically different from a zero correlation: $r = -.17$, $p = .35$ (note the negative sign of the correlation coefficient r and the associated p value which is greater than .05). That is, we cannot exclude the possibility that there is no systematic relationship between the cut effect and semantic distance as measured by BERT.

What these differential correlation patterns mean concretely can be gleaned from looking at a few 'exemplary' poems — see Figure 2. Figure 2 shows two poems of the context–action type (upper row) and two of the juxtaposition type (lower row); the haiku on the left have relatively low similarity between fragment and phrase (near-equivalent semantic similarity scores of .38/.37 for the context–action/juxtaposition haiku), and those to the right have relatively high similarity (scores of .59/.59). Superimposed on the text in each line of the haiku is a 'heat map' illustrating how much time the eye spent overall on each word, or word part, within the line: hotter (redder) colors denote more time (measured in milliseconds: msec). In all haiku depicted, the cut is positioned between lines 1 and 2 (i.e., line 1 is the fragment and lines 2 and 3 are the phrase).

As can be seen, in "hospital ward / at last moonlight / fades into dawn" (S. Pelter), the cut effect is small even though the semantic similarity is low. Conversely, in "first cold morning / the smell of mothballs / on her jersey" (P. Prime), the cut effect is large even though the semantic similarity is high. For the two juxtaposition haiku depicted, the relationship is exactly the other way round: the cut effect is larger for the haiku with the greater semantic distance, i.e., for "prenuptial contract / fish bones neatly spaced / on white china" (R. C. Moss) as compared to "the sound of the sea / speaking to my mother/ on her birthday" (L. Rees). Recall, however, that this negative relationship between semantic similarity and the cut effect was not significant for the whole sample of juxtaposition haiku.[7]

---

7. Of note, conclusions based on the comparison of single, 'exemplary'

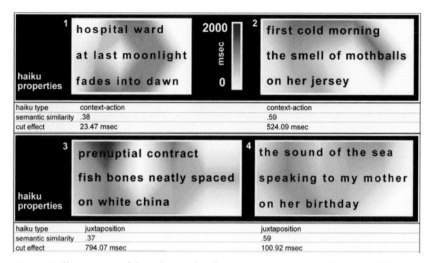

Figure 2: Illustration of the relationship between semantic similarity and the cue effect for 2 context-action haiku (upper row) and 2 juxtaposition haiku (lower row) used in Geyer et al. (see text for explanations). The corresponding haiku are marked by filled blue and, respectively, filled green circles in Figure 1.

Another noteworthy finding is that the mean semantic similarity between fragment and phrase is actually comparable between the context–action and juxtaposition haiku in our sample: .55 vs. .55 ($p = .90$). This is contrary to the hypothesis that similarity would be higher for context–action haiku. However, although there is no overall difference, the similarity scores show higher variability in semantic similarity between fragment and phrase lines for our

---

haiku are beset with difficulty (and may be misleading), as a number of linguistically potentially important factors – such as word frequency, the ratio of content to function words, the position and form of realization (finite, infinite, ellipted) of the verb, occurrence of phoric elements like pronouns or definite determiners, etc., which all influence eye-fixation duration — would likely be uncontrolled. This is why we have advocated an approach comparing sets of (individual) haiku of a particular type, which we can equate (and did equate in Geyer et al. and thus the data re-examined for the purposes of the present study) in terms of these factors at the sample level.

sample of juxtaposition haiku, compared to the context–action haiku. This may be seen by comparing the two panels in Figure 1: the individual poems cluster less densely around the mean with juxtaposition than with context–action haiku. We tested this statistically by computing the standard deviation[8] of the poems' similarity scores within each haiku set: this measure turned out significantly higher for juxtaposition than for context–action haiku: .10 vs. .07 ($p = .04$).

Thus, taken together, these results of our exploratory analyses are interesting. However, because they run counter to what was expected in several respects, any attempt to explain them is necessarily 'post hoc' at this stage. Nevertheless, we offer a few speculations.

To recap, the most important finding was that semantic similarity, as measured by BERT, cannot account for the differential cut effects between our context–action and juxtaposition haiku; further, semantic similarity appears to play a different role for the two types of haiku. For context–action haiku, the relationship between the cut effect and semantic similarity is positive: the cut effect is the larger, the smaller (rather than the larger) the distance between the fragment and phrase images. This seems to suggest that it is not the difficulty of retrieving a fitting cut-resolving schema (of the context–action variety) from memory that is critical for the cut effect. But perhaps, on the contrary, when the fragment and phrase images are semantically closer, multiple possible (concrete) resolution schemas may be retrieved, so that it becomes harder to settle on one. That is, when the semantic distance is smaller, a greater variety of specific images are evoked by the phrase (action) and/or the fragment (context), providing a larger space of how the

8. The standard deviation is a measure of the variability, or spread of a distribution, of data points around the mean: for normally distributed variables ca. 68% of all data points lie within the range mean plus/minus one standard deviation.

action may be grounded within the context. As a result, there may be more competition between simultaneously active but conflicting interpretations, and the increased difficulty of the resolution is expressed in the extended processing of the fragment image. Alternatively, multiple 'readings' may be maintained concurrently (without settling on one solution), and it is this which is reflected in the increased cut effect. Of course, these two possibilities would not be mutually exclusive: which one applies depends on the particular poem and reader.

For juxtaposition haiku, by contrast, we found no robust systematic relationship between semantic distance and the cut effect. Of note, though, (at least) the poems in our sample of juxtaposition haiku exhibited a greater spread (variability) of their associated similarity scores compared to context–action haiku, likely reflecting the fact that the conceptual structure of juxtaposition haiku is more heterogeneous compared to context–action haiku (which can all be subsumed under one general, context–action schema). As a result, with juxtaposition haiku, readers have less opportunity to draw on a repertoire of a readily available (previously acquired) schemata compared to juxtaposition haiku, and a greater degree of 'lateral thinking' is required to come up with a solution that bridges the gap between the two images. While there was some weak evidence of finding and settling on one solution becoming easier with increasing semantic similarity between the phrase and fragment images (i.e., the cut effect tended to decrease with increasing semantic similarity), it could be that, at the high similarity end, some haiku may invoke multiple resolutions (increasing competition and thus the cut effect, as with context–action haiku), whereas at the low similarity end the disparate images force a sudden 'insight' solution for some haiku. Such processes would wash out a general semantic similarity effect (rendering the correlation non-significant).

To conclude, our initial analyses indicate that 'semantic similarity' — as least as measured by state-of-the-art neural network models — does not readily (without extra assumptions) explain the cut effect, neither for context–action haiku for which we found a positive (rather than the expected negative) correlation, nor for juxtaposition haiku for which we found no correlation (though there was a slight trend towards a negative correlation). We offered some speculations of how these patterns may be explained, but these would need to be corroborated by further work (elaborating their implications and testing the predictions deriving from these).

Computational measures of semantic similarity based on neural network models have proven psychological validity. For instance, they are superior to other (e.g., judgment-based) measures in accounting for a large body of 'semantic priming' effects[9] reported in the literature (see Mandera et al. for a recent review). However, our results suggest that similarity metrics based on distributional semantic representations account for only a small fraction of the observed variation in the cut effect, which we take to be a marker of how readers come to understand haiku. Thus, for semantic accounts to have greater explanatory potential with respect to the reading of haiku (and perhaps poetry in general), we propose that, at the least, they would need to be extended by the notion of more comprehensive, conceptually organizing 'cognitive structures' (Talmy, "Toward a Cognitive Semantics"; see also Jacobs) which, when integrated with (potentially disparate) conceptual contents, give rise to unified cognitive representations — in our case: the 'meaning Gestalt' (Iser) of a haiku. Further, semantic accounts may have to acknowledge that language experience alone cannot

9. 'Semantic priming' refers to the finding that reading for instance the word 'space' facilitates the processing of the later word 'astronaut', which in turn narrows the meaning potential of the prior 'space'. These influences are explained through spreading activation, in feedforward and feedback direction, among conceptual nodes in semantic networks (e.g., Collins & Loftus).

be the (sole) basis of our semantic-conceptual system (Glenberg & Robertson); rather, our theorizing needs to incorporate notions of 'embodied' or 'grounded' cognition' (e.g., Barsalou, "Perceptual symbol systems"; Barsalou, "Grounded cognition"; Zwaan & Madden) to better capture our rich and 'situated' perceptual (multi-sensory), emotional, aesthetic, and (inter-)action-based experience of the world. If conceptualized in this way, measures of 'cognitive-semantic disparity' may have greater potential to gauge how wide the gap is between a haiku's juxtaposed images and how the reader brings them together in an attentive, Gestalt-creating process.

The shortcomings of current artificial neural networks, such as BERT, in capturing and truly understanding the semantic content of deeper conceptual constructs as found in haiku (and perhaps poetic language in general) are likely owing to the fact that they cannot (yet) be trained on similarly rich types of inputs. This is because there is still a gap between the purely 'language-based' domain, where fully implemented computational models are available, and the more 'perception-based' domain, where notions and conceptual entities of grounded cognition are still not sufficiently formalized to be implemented computationally. This gap has been acknowledged in the literature (e.g., Pezzulo et al.) and has led to attempts to develop artificial neural networks that map out, for example, the space of visual representations, enabling them to capture the similarity between complex visual images. In the longer run, such developments may yield neural network models that have greater explanatory value with regard to how we understand poetic texts.

Of course, beyond such more 'grounded' semantic representations, there is also the transactional side in reading haiku — that is, poems that encapsulate the 'haiku moment' experienced by the poet, which may be re-experienced by the reader in an interpersonal process of sharing. Awareness of the writer, who had the insight and communicates it, is likely to be a central element in the reader's appreciation of a haiku. Future work may show whether this aspect is amenable to modeling or whether it will remain a mystery.

References

Allen, Melissa. "Bruised Apples." *Acorn* 26 (2011).

Antonio, Billy. Closing My Eyes." *The Heron's Nest*, vol. 17, no. 1, 2015, p. 4. www.theheronsnest.com/March2015/haiku-p4.html. Accessed 23 September 2020.

Barsalou, Lawrence W. "Perceptual Symbol Systems." *Behavioral and Brain Sciences*, vol. 22, 1999, pp. 637–660.

Barsalou, Lawrence W. "Grounded Cognition". *Annual Review of Psychology*, vol. 59, 2008, pp. 617–645.

Collins, Allan M., and Elizabeth F. Loftus. "A Spreading-Activation Theory of Semantic Processing." *Psychological Review*, vol. 82, 1975, pp. 407–428.

Devlin, Jacob, Ming-Wei Chang, Kenton Lee and Kristina Toutanova. "BERT: Pre-training of deep bidirectional transformers for language understanding." arXiv:1810.04805v2 [cs.CL], 018. Accessed 23 September 2020.

Firth, John R. "A Synopsis of Linguistic Theory 1930–1955." *Studies in Linguistic Analysis*, edited by J. R. Firth, Basil Blackwell, 1957, pp. 1–32.

Geyer, Thomas, Franziska Günther, Jim Kacian, Heinrich R. Liesefeld, Hermann J. Müller and Stella Pierides. "Reading English-language Haiku: An Eye-Movement Study of the 'Cut Effect." *Journal of Eye Movement Research*, vol. 13 no. 2, 2020, pp. 1–29 DOI: https://doi.org/10.16910/jemr.13.2.2. Accessed 23 September 2020.

Glenberg, Arthur M., and David A. Robertson. "Symbol Grounding and Meaning: A Comparison of High-Dimensional and Embodied Theories of Meaning." *Journal of Memory and Language*, vol. 43, 2000, pp. 379–401.

Iser, Wolfgang. Der Akt des Lesens. *Theorie der ästhetischen Erfahrung*. München: Fink (1976).

Jacobs, Arthur M. (2015). "Neurocognitive Poetics: Methods and Models for Investigating the Neuronal and Cognitive-Affective Bases of Literature Reception." *Frontiers in Human Neuroscience*, vol. 9:186, 2015, pp. 1–22. DOI: doi.org/10.3389/fnhum.2015.00186. Accessed 23 September 2020.

Just, Marcel A., and Patricia A. Carpenter. "A Theory of Reading: From Eye Fixations to Comprehension." *Psychological Review*, vol. 87, no. 4, 1980, pp. 329–354.

Kacian, Jim. *How to Haiku*. Winchester, VA: Red Moon Press (2006).

Langacker, Ronald W. *Cognitive Grammar: A Basic Introduction*. Oxford, UK: Oxford University Press (2008).

Liddy, Elizabeth D. "Natural Language Processing". *Encyclopedia of Library and Information Science* (2nd edition), edited by Miriam A. Drake, Marcel Dekker, 2001. https://surface.syr.edu/istpub/63/. Accessed 23 September 2020.

Mandera, Pawel, Emmanuel Keuleers and Marc Brysbaert. "Explaining Human Performance in Psycholinguistic Tasks with Models of Semantic Similarity Based on Prediction and Counting: A Review and Empirical Validation." *Journal of Memory and Language*, vol. 92, 2017, pp. 57–78.

Moss, Ron C. "Prenuptial Contract." *Acorn*, vol. 30, 2013.

Pelter, Stanley. "Hospital Ward." *Dust of Summers*, Red Moon Press (2007).

Pezzulo, Giovanni, Lawrence W. Barsalou, Angelo Cangelosi, Martin H. Fischer, Michael J. Spivey and Ken McRae (2011). "The Mechanics of Embodiment: A Dialog on Embodiment and Computational Modeling." *Frontiers in Psychology*, vol. 2, 2011 pp.

1–21. DOI: 10.3389/fpsyg.2011.00005. Accessed 23 September 2020.

Pierides, Stella, Thomas Geyer, Franziska Günther, Jim Kacian, Heinrich R. Liesefeld and Hermann J. Müller. "Knocking on the Doors of Perception. Further Inquiries into Haiku and the Brain." *Juxtapositions: A Journal of Haiku Research and Scholarship*, vol. 5, 2019, pp. 9–33. www.thehaikufoundation.org/juxta/juxta-5-1/knocking-on-the-doors-of-perception-further-inquiries-into-haiku-and-the-brain/. Accessed 23 September 2020.

Prime, Patricia. "First cold morning." S. Chauhan (ed.), *Beyond the Fields*. Aesthetics Publications (2017).

Rees, Lynne (2009). "The Sound of the Sea." 2nd With Words International Online Haiku Competition (2nd prize) (2009). URL: www.withwords.org.uk/results.html

Talmy, Leonard. "Fictive Motion in Language and 'Caption.'" *Language and Space*, edited by P. Bloom, M. A. Petersen, L. Nadel, & M. F. Garret, MIT Press, 1996, pp. 211–276.

Talmy, Leonard. *Toward a Cognitive Semantics. Vol. 1: Concept Structuring Systems. Vol. 2: Typology and Process in Concept Structuring*. Cambridge, MA: MIT Press (2000).

Van Peer, Wille, J. Hakemulder and S. Zyngier. "Lines on Feeling: Foregrounding, Aesthetics and Meaning." *Language and Literature*, vol. 16, 2007, pp. 197–213.

Zwaan, Rolf A., and Carrol J. Madden. "Embodied Sentence Comprehension." *Grounding Cognition: The Role of Action and Perception in Memory, Language, and Thinking*, edited by D. Pecher & R. A. Zwaan, Cambridge University Press, 2005, pp. 224–245.

dry flowers —
a butterfly makes
its farewells

Poet/Artist: Ion Codrescu

Richard Wright's
Haiku: This Other World

A Making Procedure

Toru Kiuchi

ABSTRACT: Richard Wright's *Haiku: This Other World*, a collection of 817 haiku, edited by Yoshinobu Hakutani and Robert L. Tener, was published by Arcade in 1998. The manuscript was already completed by Wright in 1960 but long remained unpublished since Wright's untimely death in 1960. It was then deposited by Ellen Wright, wife of Richard Wright, to Beinecke Rare Book and Manuscript Library of Yale University in 1976. The access to the manuscript was restricted at the library but Ellen Wright responded to Tener's letter, suggesting in 1986 that he and Hakutani work with her toward the publication of the manuscript. The library finally allowed Hakutani and Tener "to read it in its entirety in the spring of 1991" (Wright, Haiku xiii-xiv). In 1998 Hakutani and Tener thus published the collection of Wright's haiku under the title of *Haiku: This Other World* with the introduction by Julia Wright, daughter of Richard Wright, and editors' "Notes on the Haiku" and "Afterword." There is a long procedure from Wright's engagement with Japan to his encounter with haiku through the composition of haiku. Wright's expertise of Japan and Japanese culture unfolds by reading newspaper articles, confronting political groups, making use of the country for fiction, and meeting real-life Japanese. In later years after acquirement of the previous knowledge of Zen-like African philosophy, he runs across haiku, by which he is immediately possessed, while suffering from a disease. There are five stages of his composition of haiku from his prolific and experimental writing of haiku to meticulous revision to the change of arrangement of haiku from season to theme through the final draft. Especially, it is notable that in the course of the selection and relinquishment of haiku, its arrangement changes from season to theme at the suggestion of a Japanese professor. The final draft has the arrangement of themes but the published version is slightly different from that. This essay pursues the development from Wright's interest in Japan to his composition of haiku through the posthumous publication.

I. Engagement with Japan

Before his encounter with haiku, the genesis of Wright's interest in the style of poetry can be found in his engagement with Japan where haiku was born in the 16th century. The first time when Japan enters Wright's consciousness is probably in September 1923 when fourteen-year-old Wright reads articles about Japan in the *Chicago Defender* in Jackson, Mississippi because one of Wright's after-school jobs is to deliver the *Chicago Defender* in which he notices the news of the great earthquake in Japan (Rowley 32).[1] Wright leaves Jackson for Memphis, Tennessee in 1925 and finds a job as an assistant and delivery boy at the American Optical Company in October. Wright reads articles in *Argosy* detailing Japanese atrocities in occupied China ("The Pulp Magazines Project") as his boss Edwin E. Shroyer, Sr. proves: "I remember that he used to read a lot, particularly the *Argosy* magazine and a lot of books" (Ray and Farnsworth 23). In Chicago in summer 1929 Wright, twenty-one years old, praises Marcus Garvey (1887 – 1940) who applauds Japan as a model nation for African Americans and as a leader of

---

1. The Great Kantō earthquake struck the Kantō Plain on the main Japanese island of Honshū on 1 September 1923 with 105,385 deaths confirmed in the quake. The *Chicago Defender* spread the news all over: "The [Chicago] *Defender* promptly launched such a campaign" (Kearney 122). The newspaper deployed an energetic campaign for the disaster in Japan: "The *Defender* [15 September 1923] asked its readers to 'make a creditable showing.' None of us are so poor that we cannot give something to such 'a worthy cause,' the *Defender* admonished the hesitant" (Kearney 123). Not only the earthquake but also the discriminatory treatment of Japanese which leads to racism against African Americans might have drawn Wright's attention when he possibly saw the cartoon in the front page of the newspaper: "On April 19, 1924, the *Chicago Defender* ran a front page cartoon in which a brick hurled by a California land owner labelled 'Land Shall Be Sold to Caucasians Only' bounced off a Japanese and hit a black American" (Hellwig 93).

people of color (Fabre, *Quest* 81).[2] In 1937 Wright, now twenty-nine years old, leaves Chicago for New York where he becomes a reporter for *Daily Worker*, a newspaper for the Communist Party, and writes articles about Japan.[3]

Three years later in 1940 Bigger Thomas, protagonist in Wright's bestseller novel *Native Son* as a misanthrope, serves as a mouthpiece for an admirer of Japan: "He [Bigger Thomas] liked to hear of how Japan was conquering China" (98).[4] Five years later in 1945 Amy Tory, a young second-generation Japanese American, proves Wright's keener interest in Japan with a lot of questions on her.[5] Two years later Wright leaves New York for Paris in August 1947.

Cross Damon, protagonist in an existential novel *The Outsider* (1953) and another mouthpiece for Wright, refers to Japan as an industrially overripe nation who is moving away from a traditional

---

2. The Garveyite group Wright meets praises Japan and enthralls him as an international organization: "The Garveyites had embraced a totally racialistic outlook which endowed them with a dignity that I had never seen before in Negroes. On the walls of their dingy flats were maps of Africa and India and Japan, pictures of Japanese generals and admirals, portraits of Marcus Garvey in gaudy regalia, the faces of colored men and women from all parts of the world" (*Black Boy* [*American Hunger*] 336).
3. Wright's some anti-Japanese articles are such as "Harlem Party to Protest Japan's Action" (27 July 1937), "Picket Lines Win Withdrawal of All Goods Made in Japan" (1 November 1937), and "Pickets Force Stores to Ban Japan Goods" (30 November 1937).
4. Wright's interest in Asia leads to his writing of a letter to Department of State on 13 May 1941, requesting a passport to be a foreign correspondent in Japan, Russia, and other countries. The procedure is detailed in Kiuchi's "Zen" (25).
5. Wright's 14 January 1945 journal records that she is all afternoon probed "for some idea, some notion, some attitude toward life that escapes the stock-in-trade answers" (Kiuchi, "Zen" 26).

and simple way of life.[6] From June to September 1953 Wright travels around the Gold Coast (later Ghana) in West Africa. Wright's revelation during his trip to the African country is that the African "primal outlook upon life," which is based upon the Akan religion of the Ashanti, is fundamentally different from the Western outlook on life, but similar to Eastern philosophy. The experiences encourage Wright to later realize that the African religion is akin to Zen Buddhism in haiku.[7]

Wright's stay in Indonesia from 12 April to 4 May 1955 to attend the Bandung Conference (18-24 April 1955) is most pivotal and enlightening. Some Japanese are Wright's acquaintances but they are all Japanese living outside Japan.[8] Wright has a rare chance to meet a Japanese newspaper reporter there.[9] In Jakarta, Indonesia, Wright is placed in the same accommodation with another Japanese

---

6. Cross Damon states in the novel: "I'm referring to nations like England, Japan, Germany, etc. In these nations the problem of the future structure of society and the question of what kind of faith will sustain the individual in his daily life constitute a kind of chronic spiritual terror" (*The Outsider* 353).

7. According to Hakutani, "the 'primal outlook upon life,' as he [Wright] called it, served as an inspiration for his poetic sensibility" (Wright and Haiku 131). A reading of Wright's haiku, argues Hakutani, indicates that "Wright turned away from the moral, intellectual, social, and political problems dealt with in his prose work and found in nature his latent poetic sensibility" (Wright and Haiku 132).

8. Ellen Wright's sister-in-law is one of them — Ellen's brother Martin in Pearl Harbor, Hawaii writes Wright on 25 January 1945, saying that he is going to marry a native Japanese girl (Journal, Yale) but Wright does not have a chance to meet her frequently.

9. On the way to Bandung, Wright takes a plane from Karachi, Pakistan to Calcutta, India to Jakarta, Indonesia and gets into a conversation with a Japanese newspaperman: "Despite his bookish English, he made me understand that he was terribly interested in Africa" (*The Color Curtain* 75-81).

journalist (Roberts and Foulcher 68). Especially the speech at the conference by Tatsunosuke Takasaki (1885–1964), a principal Japanese delegate at the Conference,[10] is impressive and agreeable to Wright because Takasaki's attitude is modest and "he had to speak in a confessional tone" apologizing to Asian countries for what she has done during World War II (*The Color Curtain* 149). After the conference Wright is well received as the houseguest for some ten days by Fujiko Yamanaka (1908–1959), an American-born Japanese wife of Winburn T. Thomas (1909–1981), a missionary in Jakarta whose knowledge of Japan is deep and accurate [11] (Roberts and Foulcher 95).[12] In his later years in 1959, with such a knowledge of Japan, Wright runs across and begins to write haiku in Paris through his illness and loneliness.

II. Encounter with Haiku

Wright's illness begins in Paris from 1 July 1959 at the age of fifty-one according to the letter to his literary agent Reynolds: "From the first of July I've been undergoing heavy medication and it makes me as weak as a kitten" (Wright to Reynolds, 14 September, qtd.

10. Takasaki was a great man who saved millions of Japanese people's lives at the end of WWII. Millions of general Japanese in Manchuria were left behind without means of coming home to Japan because the Manchuria government and the army were under arrest and killed by China and the Soviet Union in August 1945. So Takasaki, just a president of a company, desperately negotiated with Chinese companies to charter boats to send back home millions of Japanese.

11. Thomas was in Kyoto, Japan as a missionary from 1932-1940 and published Protestant Beginnings in Japan (Tokyo: Charles E. Tuttle, 1959), a Ph.D dissertation from Yale University, covering the first three decades of Protestantism in Japan, 1859-1889.

12. On 9 July 1959 Wright sends a letter of condolence to Thomas, expressing his sympathy with Fujiko's death in Chicago (Thomas to Wright, 23 July 1959, Yale).

Fabre, Quest 619n15). He is in a bad state of health for a month and spends a week from 22 to 29 August (Entry arrangement card, Yale) at the American Hospital in Paris (Fabre, Quest 492). The diagnosis is amoebic dysentery. The doctors think that he probably caught the amoebae from contaminated food in West Africa, a high-risk area (Rowley 501). At the same time Ellen and his daughters Julia and Rachel move to London on temporary visas without Wright, and for the time being Ellen rents a house in London (Rowley 498, 587n57). Illness and loneliness sometimes urge people to write haiku as Wright says: "I made a strange use of my illness and produced something" (Wright to Reynolds, 6 April 1960, Yale). Haiku require less energy than short stories and novels because they are written only in three lines; loneliness is one of the states of mind which the creation and appreciation of haiku demand.[13]

Sinclair Beiles (1930–2000), a South African Beat poet, lives in a hotel—the Beat Hotel at 9 rue Git-le-Coeur in the Latin Quarter in Paris. The Beat poets who gather at the Beat Hotel are quite interested in Zen; likewise, the Beat Generation writers are attracted to Zen and haiku as testified by books by Jack Kerouac (1922–1969) such as *The Dharma Bums* (1958), *Satori in Paris* (1966), to say nothing of *Book of Haikus*[14] (2003). Because Wright is already familiar with Japanese culture and interested in Zen Buddhism, he meets Beiles through the interest in Africa and Zen by way of the introduction of Albert Camus or Jean-Paul Sartre and other Beat poets at the Beat Hotel close to his apartment at rue Monsieur le Prince in late August 1959. There, he enjoys talking

---

13. Blyth notes in the volume one of his *Haiku*: "Sabishisa, loneliness, is the haiku equivalent of *Mu* in Zen, a state of absolute spiritual poverty in which, having nothing, we possess all" (I: 162).

14. Haiku is both singular and plural. Kerouac's usage of "s" is the same as Wright's.

with Beiles about Africa, Zen, and Japanese culture before Beiles happens to mention haiku.

Wright is immediately fascinated by haiku and starts to attempt writing it by borrowing from Beiles the four volumes of *Haiku* by R. H. Blyth on the art of haiku, and learning the composition method from the book (Fabre, Quest 505). Wright begins to write haiku in late August 1959 and stops it in mid-March 1960, starting first from creating Earliest Draft comprising of about 4,000 haiku then to revision through five stages.

III. Five Stages

1st stage — Earliest Draft

From late August 1959, as soon as good haiku pop up in his mind, Wright writes them in longhand and sends them to a Canadian typist to have her typewrite them on loose-leaf papers, one verse on each leaf. The typist comes to his apartment for a few hours a day, two or three times a week (Fabre, Quest 508). Wright writes about twenty haiku a day on the average at breakneck pace. Wright continues to work hard in fall 1959 in spite of the disease and casually speaks over lunch about the possibility of the publication of haiku to William Targ, a World Publishing editor, who is in Paris (Wright to Reynolds, 6 April 1960, qtd. Fabre, Quest 620n24). Temporarily out of the hospital at the end of August, Wright writes haiku:

> While convalescing,
> The red roses have no smell,
> Gently mocking me. (224)[15]

15. The number does not signify the page number but the numbering on each haiku done by Hakutani and Tener in *Haiku: This Other World*, which is, one should note, different from any numbering in Earliest

Julia Wright recalls her father's crafting of haiku:

> One of my last memories of my father during the summer and autumn months before he died is his crafting of thousands of haiku. He was never without his haiku binder under his arm. He wrote them everywhere, at all hours: in bed as he slowly recovered from a year-long, grueling battle against amebic dysentery; in cafés and restaurants where he counted syllables on napkins; ... I remember how he would hang pages and pages of them up, as if to dry, on long metal rods strung across the narrow office area of his tiny sunless studio in Paris...I also recall how one day he tried to teach me how to count the syllables: "Julia, you can write them, too. It's always five, and seven and five—like math. So you can't go wrong." (Wright, Haiku vii-viii)

Wright therefore does not forget to write haiku on his fifty-first birthday on 4 September 1959:

> It is September
> The month in which I was born
> And I have no thoughts. (508)

Wright's tone in haiku is pessimistic while still under heavy medication in September according to his avowal: "I've had to undergo heavy and prolonged medication and am now seeming to be pulling out" (Wright to Winslow, 11 September, FPC):

> This September rain
> Is much colder than the wind
> That sweeps it along. (279)

Wright's health permits him to travel to London again in mid-September (Fabre, Quest 493), so Wright boards the Channel

---

Draft, Notebooks (1) and (2), Working Drafts (1) and (2), Cardboard Draft, and Final Draft.

ferry at Boulogne, France on 16 September and is told to give his passport to the British authorities until he arrives at Folkestone in England. When the ferry docks at Folkstone, he is kept waiting for more than one hour and is asked many times whether or not he intends to reside in England this time (Wright to Strachey, 12 October, FPC). He is finally let go on one-week visitor's visa and fills out a landing card (Fabre, Quest 494), giving free vent to his pent-up feelings in the following:

> The crowded harbor:
> Soft lights are blazing at dawn
> In a drizzling rain. (390)

When Wright is in London between 17-19 September, Ellen Wright buys a copy of R. H. Blyth's *Haiku* at the request of her husband, who is still using a set of Blyth's book borrowed from Beiles (Fabre, Books & Writers 14) and, for most of his stay in England, writes haiku like the following on his bed, too weak to go out with a disease (Rowley 501):

> Tossing all day long,
> The cold sea now sleeps deeply
> On a bed of stars. (196)

At the request of Gunnar Myrdal (1898–1987), Wright's friend and a Nobel laureate, Edita Morris[16] (1902–1988) tries to help Wright financially with his plan to visit French West Africa,

---

16. Her husband Ira Morris (1903–1972), who comes from a wealthy family background, founded a rest house in Hiroshima for victims of the bomb. In October 1959 what with Gunnar Myrdal's efforts to raise funds having failed, and the news that Ira Morris, who at this time is supporting liberal pacifist movements and is one of Wright's last hopes, can be of no help to him, the plan was to go to French West Africa (Fabre, Quest 491). On 6 October 1959 Myrdal writes to Wright telling him that he received a negative letter from Ira Morris.

partially associating Africa with haiku in the plan[17] but is not successful because her foundation has already committed all the funds to the Hiroshima project (Myrdal to Wright, 6 October, Yale). Edita then inscribes to Wright as a token of apology a copy of her novel *The Flowers of Hiroshima*, just published in September by Viking Press (Fabre, Books & Writers, 112). Wright reads Morris's book, impressed with the atrocities of Hiroshima, Japan. Morris is mostly known for her novel which is partly influenced by the experiences of her son, Ivan Morris.[18] The novel leads to the lines in Wright's unpublished haiku, "When the jet bombers flew past" (leaf number 664, Earliest Draft, Yale) and "Not one bombing plane" (leaf number 2034, Earliest Draft, Yale).

Wright's good friend George Padmore (1903–1959), a Pan-Africanist and author of Pan-Africanism or Communism? *The Coming Struggle for Africa* (1956) with a foreword by Wright, passes away in London at the age of fifty-six on 23 September (New York Times, 25 September) right after Wright comes back to Paris from London, so Wright immediately flies back to London from Paris to attend Padmore's funeral (Fabre, Quest 494) on 29 September and writes haiku:

---

17. Wright finishes typing the seventy-two-page manuscript of "French West Africa" on 12 May 1959 (box 5, folder 86, Yale), looking for the fund of Wright's research in French West Africa. "Ideas for French Africa" on 49 points to be checked and things to be done mostly in connection with this second African project. One of the items to be done is "26. What about interlacing HAIKUS in text?"

18. Ivan Morris (1925-1976), later a distinguished Japanologist, is an intelligence officer in the U.S. Navy visiting Hiroshima immediately after the dropping of the atomic bomb on the city. Edita and Ira Morris visited Hiroshima in 1955 and decided to create a facility where the survivors could get some peace of mind.

At a funeral,
Strands of filmy spider webs
On coffin flowers. (482)

Wright sells the apartment on rue Monsieur le Prince on 30
October after living there for twelve years and buys a two-room
apartment on the ground floor of rue Régis (Fabre, Quest 493).
Wright's amoebic dysentery is still being treated on 1 November
but his doctor allows him to work only on the condition that he lie
down the minute he is tired with haiku (Fabre, Quest 496):

Leaving the doctor,
The whole world looks different
This autumn morning. (243)

A young Japanese girlfriend, Mary Oké, cooks for Wright at times
at the new small apartment. Mary could give her suggestion for
Wright's haiku from her native Japanese point of view. Wright's
friend Harrington describes Wright's newly rented small apartment
as he sees it: "The other side of the living room is almost completely
occupied by a tremendous glass-doored bookcase containing
copies of Richard Wright in languages ranging from Japanese to
Turkish . . ." (14). Wright's haiku is written beside the Japanese
version of *Uncle Tom's Children*[19] on the bookcase:

Merciful autumn
Tones down the shabby curtains
Of my rented room. (174)

Wright's haiku is still written out of illness to comfort his lonely
mind (Wright to Reynolds, 11 December, FPC):

---

19. On 4 November 1955 Harper & Brothers sent Wright "quite a beautiful
book," a copy of the Japanese translation of *Uncle Tom's Children*, published
by Shinchosha of Tokyo (Firestone Library, Princeton University).

An empty sickbed:
An indented white pillow
In weak winter sun. (425)

In mid-December Wright leaves for the Moulin d'Andé[20] in Normandy to spend relaxed days, listening to the radio, eating, sleeping, and taking drives in his car. Wright writes haiku during the day he lies on his bed or sits quietly, like an old man (Rowley 505):

A December wind
Swept the sky clean of clouds
And froze the lake still. (65)

Wright is thus possessed by haiku: "Images of Normandy fog, church bells, scarecrows, and cows tangle with images of magnolias, cornstalks, and cotton from Wright's Mississippi childhood" (Rowley 505-06):

From a cotton field
To magnolia trees,
A bridge of swallows. (725)

Wright returns to Paris from the Moulin d'Andé on 25 December to share a Christmas with his family, who came back from London (Fabre, Quest 497). His haiku is cynical as he does not seem to enjoy the occasion to the full:

For six dark dank years,
A doll with a Christmas smile
In an old shoe box. (588)

---

20. The Moulin d'Andé, where Wright haunts to meditate to write haiku, an old flour mill not far from Rouen, which is about 75 miles northwest of Paris (Fabre, Quest 497).

Wright's haiku is like the following after Christmas when his family leaves for London and rain in the morning changes to snow at night on 1 January 1960:

> All the city's bells
> Clang deafeningly this midnight,
> Frightening the New Year! (183)

The number of haiku by Wright now amounts to about 3,050 in early January 1960, according to the report in the letter to his girlfriend Celia Hornung: "I've reached 3,050 haikus!" He reports further: "I'm alone, so alone, so I write haikus. Maybe one in ten will be good or of some use" (Wright to Hornung, 12 January, FPC) and writes 250 more between 12 and 19 January.

The number of haiku amounts to 3,300 in late January: "I've reached Haiku number 3,300; I'm almost now through with 'em; Three or four hundred more and I'll call it quits. I think that I now really understand them and I've gotten a hell of a lot out of studying them" (Wright to Hornung, 19 January, FPC).

The first day of spring 1960 is 4 February when Wright writes haiku:

> The first day of spring:
> The snow on the far mountains,
> Brighter than ever. (173)

The number of haiku grows from 3,300 in early January to 3,700 in early February as reported in the letter to Hornung: "Am alone. See nobody. Walk the streets and look and long and yearn. . . . I've got to Haiku 3,700 and stopped. . . . I'll go over them sometime soon" (Wright to Hornung, 5 February, FPC). The development of his haiku is inevitably like the following since the average rainfall during February in Paris is essentially constant:

> How lonely it is:
> A winter world full of rain,
> Rain raining on rain. (319)

The number of haiku increases more by 300 between early February and mid-March, reaching about 4,000. Wright writes to Hornung that he stops writing them and starts to select good ones from them: "Haiku number 4,000. The end for the moment. I've actually stopped writing them. I went over the lot and picked out 1066 to try to do something with. I had not thought that I'd find so many that I liked" (Wright to Hornung, 16 March, FPC).

Thus Earliest Draft consisting of 4,000 haiku, systematically with one verse typewritten on each loose leaf [Beinecke librarian put together one hundred loose leaves in each folder, making forty folders] (boxes 71-78, folders 838-877, Yale) is created in mid-March. As a matter of fact, the exact total haiku number of Early Draft is 3,998 because of five missing leaves (85, 173, 427, 435, and 445) and three additional leaves (2623a, 3707a, and 3707b).

2nd stage—Notebooks (1) and (2)

Wright writes to his Dutch translator and friend Margrit de Sablonière (1905 – 1979), who lives in Leiden, Holland, telling her that all the doctors who see him say that his condition is not so bad but that he does not get used to it because he does not just sit around but is used to continuous action, and asking her whether Shibika,[21] a Japanese professor at Leiden University, can check the value of his haiku when he goes to Leiden in late April: "Is the man, Prof. Shibika, a Japanese? If so, maybe he would like to see the stuff I've done, but it is all in English. There is a typist who comes in for a couple of hours, two or three times a week; soon I may have 800 or 1000 ready to be looked at" (Wright to Sablonière, 24

---

21. This cannot be a Japanese name; maybe Shibaki.

March, FPC). Because he does not have friends who are familiar with this special type of poems, haiku, so Sablonière's suggestion to introduce a Japanese professor is quite welcome to Wright so that he can rely on the judgment of his haiku from the viewpoint of a native Japanese. Wright accepts her offer, asking her again to wait for the end of selection effort: "A woman is typing up my haikus. They well may not be worth a damn. They are such fragile things, like spider webs, and I'm having none [*sic*] friends to read them and help me to decide" (Wright to Sablonière 28 March, FPC). Wright is in a great hurry to get ready for the manuscript which is to be checked by the professor in late April: "I have a girl typing up the haikus; maybe in a month they will be done, for she works for me after working all day in an office. But I like to take my time. I'll let you see the haikus when they are finished" (Wright to Sablonière, 30 March, FPC).

In early April 1960 Wright starts to select presentable haiku from Earliest Draft by putting red or blue circles at the right top of each loose leaf to send them to the typist but this time five selected verses to be typewritten on one loose leaf. The typist works hard to make Notebooks (1) and (2) following Wright's order to pick up circled leaves. Wright puts a circle on the following haiku which has the possibility of being better if corrected:

> Persistent magpies
> Are pecking amid hot grasses
> At one blue glass eye. (124)

The first line is corrected from "A persistent crow"; the second line, from "Is pecking amid wild grass"; and the third line, from "At a blue glass eye."

Wright notifies his literary agent Reynolds that he finished writing about 4,000 haiku and is soon sending them to him to ask for his opinion: "I shall send you, within a month or so, a new ms., completely different from anything I've done so far. Non-fiction. I made a strange use of my illness and produced something. Have no notion of its value, but I casually mentioned it to Bill Targ when we lunched together here in Paris last summer" (Wright to Reynolds, 6 April, Yale). Wright also writes in his letter to Sablonière: "The typing of the haikus is coming along fast. I've made a selection of 1400 out of 4000, and then will boil down that 1400 to something like 800. At last I've got them [haiku] so that I can hold them in my hands, and that means that I'm nearly finished. Strange, that I've such signs of working, eh? Almost like superstition. Or something" (Wright to Sablonière, 7 April, qtd. Fabre, Quest 620n23).

At the first stage Wright experimentally and randomly writes similar four or five haiku as he says "Maybe one in ten will be good or of some use" (Wright to Hornung, 12 January, FPC). For example, he writes five magnolia haiku in a row, remembering his childhood days in Mississippi, so-called "the Magnolia State." And then he selects one out of the four or five, sometimes changing the order of three lines to exchange the first line with the last:

> In the damp darkness,
> Croaking frogs are belching out
> The scent of magnolias. (227)

In early April Wright still needs to decrease the number to about 800, reporting to Sablonière:

> I've so far selected 1,500 haikus. I think now that I ought to boil them down to about 800 and leave them. The problem of selecting them is agonizing. I'm trying to figure out a scheme. But at last, I can carry them around in my hands. Before, they were strung on steel bars and weighed kilos . . . Now, only a pound or two. What crazy things I think of. Yet the physical weight of those haikus is an important thing to me. (Wright to Sablonière, 8 April, FPC)

Resultantly, the number of leaves on Notebook (1) amounts to 302 with five verses on each leaf except the last leaf with one verse, so the total number of haiku is 1,506 minus 16 doubly used haiku: 1,490 haiku are in Notebook (1) to be exact (box 70, folder 836, Yale). Notebook (2) (box 70, folder 837, Yale) is just a carbon copy of Notebook (1) but the order of leaves is somehow totally different. This is the 2nd stage completed in early April. Notebook (1) is put between a russet genuine leather binder so that he can hold in his hands to carry. The numbering for the verse and page on Notebooks (1) and (2) is done by the Beinecke librarian, not by Wright himself.

3rd stage — Working Drafts (1) and (2)

In early April 1960 Wright begins to pick up usable haiku and drop off conventional or ambivalent ones from Notebook (1). This time he designates the season for the haiku he picked up and sends them to the typist to have her typewrite this time fourteen verses on one piece of paper from season to season. As he realizes the importance of seasons in haiku, Wright follows Blyth's specification provided in his *Haiku*: "Up to recent years, haiku was simply the poetry of the seasons. As stated above, in a sense we can say the season of each verse is the subject, the verse leading the mind to a vast aspect of the world in space and time" (I: 336). Hence he picks up No. 794 as winter haiku:

> After the snowstorm,
> The cattle stands aimlessly,
> Blinking at whiteness. (794)

However, he discards as conventional the haiku concerning a cat which is sleeping under the roses at a moonlit night (p. 215, Notebook [1]). He picks up the following as spring haiku:

Did somebody call?
Looking over my shoulder:
Massive spring mountains. (203)

In this way Working Draft (1) is completed. Nevertheless, the season arrangement is not stable due to a precariously numerical balance, including two spring and two autumn groups, as follows: Working draft (1) comprises of "Winter" (16 pp., 213 verses), "Spring" (1) (11 pp., 154 verses), "Spring" (2) (16 pp., 218 verses), "Summer" (16 pp., 219 verses), and "Autumn" (1) (8 pp., 112 verses), "Autumn" (2) (7 pp., 73 verses) (total 74 pp., 989 verses). This is Working Draft (1) which has 913 haiku (seventy-six doubly used haiku), completed in mid-April 1960 (box 70, folder 833, Yale).

Consequently what is remarkable concerning Working Draft (1) is that it is sorted out according to season, strictly observing Blyth's more substantial stipulation: "Haiku have been for long classified according to the seasons and the subjects of the verse" (I: 337). According to Blyth's *Haiku*, with which Wright learns the technique of haiku, "There is almost always a season word in haiku" (I: 335). Wright also recognizes through Blyth the importance of four seasons in haiku: "The season may be the actual subject of the poem, that which is to be apprehended through the thing which is the ostensible subject" (I: 336).

As stated above, when he is to come to Leiden, Holland, Wright confirms Sablonière on 20 April if he can meet a Japanese professor while he is in Leiden. In order to show his haiku to the Japanese Professor, Wright, who finds it a rare and great chance to get an advice on his haiku although still not in good condition, he says in the letter to her after he decides to go meet the professor: "Well, we will be leaving here Friday [22 April 1960] morning, if the doctor's consultation permit; if not, we will leave at midday, in order to avoid the heavy traffic . . . I'm bringing my poor (800 of them!)

haikus. Maybe I'm really crazy to go to much bother, but my editor (at World's) has asked me to send him the ones I like best for the consideration. If I can chat with the Japanese professor, that would be fine" (Wright to Sablonière 20 April, FPC).

Wright is pressed for time to put Working Draft (1) in order by late April 1960 before he goes to Leiden. He then reduces the number of haiku from 913 in Working Draft (1) to 797, creating the 58-page Working Draft (2) with 14 haiku on each leaf (five haiku only on p. 58) minus 6 (double use), sorted out according to four seasons.

In consequence, the season arrangement and numerical balance in Working Draft (2) is almost excellent with about eighteen pages for each season, fourteen verses on each piece of paper: "Spring" (pp. 1-18, 252 verses), "Summer" (pp. 19-32, 196 verses), "Autumn" (pp. 33-44, 168 verses), and "Winter" (pp. 45-58, 187 verse) (box 70, folder 832, Yale). Working Draft (2) has 797 verses (six doubly used haiku).

4th stage — From Season to Theme

While in Leiden on 24 April 1960, Sablonière introduces to Wright Japanese Professor Shibaki,[22] who can give his professional opinion on the haiku in Working Draft (2) (Fabre, Quest 510). Shibaki's suggestion might have had a great impact on Wright's arrangement method. After he comes back to Paris from Leiden in late April 1960 Wright promises Sablonière to burnish Working Draft (2) more to make a perfect manuscript in accordance with the advice of Shibika: "I'm going to make a new selection of the Haikus; I'll send 800 or

22. In 1960 only a small number of Japanese were living in Leiden. Only about ten Dutch students were studying Japanese Studies at Leiden University. Frits Vos (1918 – 2000) was then Professor of Japanese and Japanese Studies at Leiden University, and Lecturer in Japanese. His wife was Japanese, Ayako Vos-Kobayashi. Probably Professor Vos introduced Shibaki to Sablonière through his wife.

1000. I'll see what comes of them. I have a Canadian girl helping me with typing and am trying to avoid all those people who hang around my neck like millstones . . ." (Wright to Sablonière 26 April, FPC). Wright begins a restart on Working Draft (2): "I'm back [at] my desk, determined now to finish up the haikus. I've made a promising start already" (Wright to Sablonière 27 April, FPC).

The Japanese professor probably suggests Wright to rethink of the season arrangement because his haiku include much more divergences of views and more important and complex essence than seasons alone. Arguably, a wide gap between the Western and the Eastern thought lies in the composition of haiku. Wright realizes that there exist much more complicated categorizations than expected, changing his mind and finding it difficult to categorize them as only four seasons as Blyth specifies in *Haiku*. Blyth himself divides the Zen state of mind for haiku into thirteen divisions in "Section II: Zen, The State of Mind for Haiku" (I: 153-238) in *Haiku*: Selflessness, Loneliness, Grateful Acceptance, Wordlessness, Non-intellectuality, Contradiction, Humour,[23] Freedom, Non-morality, Simplicity, Materiality, Love, and Courage.

Interestingly enough, in the light of Blyth's categorization, Wright similarly starts to scrawl on top of each verse in Working Draft (2): "Projection," "Other World," "Illusion," "Agreement," "Contrast," "Rel [Relation]," "Time [Timelessness]," "Animal-Human," "Absence," "Personification," "Death," "S [Sensation]," "Delicate," and so forth. Along with these handwritten themes, each haiku in Working Draft (2) has many kinds of symbols: a red square with a diagonal slash, a blue square, a yellow x, a green x, blue #, a check mark, etc. The meaning of these symbols are not clear at the moment but they are also likely to represent the quality and value of haiku.

---

23. Blyth is an English man whose spelling is English style.

Let us take No. 806 on which Wright scrawls "[This] Other World":

> The plow-split anthill
> Reveals scurrying black cities
> Under the horse's tail. (806)

"This Other World" will be later used for the main title of this manuscript, but it is still only one of the categorizations in Working Draft (2). Wright writes No. 806 from the memory of an anthill he saw in the Gold Coast, Africa in 1953. An anthill, which is spread only in the tropics such as Africa, Asia and Australia, is a mound accumulated up by ants or by termites for their nest; at the same time, it symbolizes a community congested with busy people as in Paris or London. "This Other World" indicates that the world where people living in the modern city are on the move like ants as in a far city in Europe.

The following No. 815 is also categorized under the theme of "This Other World" in Working Draft (2):

> Glittering with frost,
> A dead frog squats livingly
> In the garden path. (815)

On 27 July 1953 Wright, who makes a trip to the Gold Coast, goes to Prampram, a village about 30 miles from Accra, where he witnesses the funeral of an elder (Kiuchi and Hakutani 298) and listens to the beating drum for the funeral ritual: "The drums of state beat on, encouraging the 'dead' man to mount the steep hill of the other world. Naked black children stood about, their mouths agape in awe. Already the other world was as real to them as this one" (Black Power 235). In Africa, Wright understands, the dead live side by side with the living. In No. 815 a dead frog is alive in "This Other World" according to the Akan because Wright's understanding of the African concept of life is "suggestive of Zen's emphasis on transcending the dualism of life and death" (Hakutani, Wright and Haiku 137). Wright writes No. 815 and categorizes it as "This Other World" by following the instruction in Blyth's *Haiku*: "To the Japanese mind, there does not exist that tremendous gulf between us and God on the one hand, and animals, trees and stones on the other" (I: 150).

The following haiku in Working Draft (2) is categorized as "Projection":

> Even toy soldiers
> Perspire with weariness
> In the autumn mist. (250)

"Projection" Wright scribbles is later used for the subtitle in Final Draft. The meaning of "Projection" is, according to the Merriam-Webster's dictionary, "the externalization of blame, guilt, or responsibility for one's thoughts or actions as an unconscious mechanism to defend the ego against anxiety." If one projects feelings or ideas on to other people, one imagines that they have the same ideas or feelings as someone else. Wright intends No. 250 for toy soldiers to perspire with weariness instead of Wright to sweat with fever caused by illness. "This Other World" and "Projection," just ones of the categories in Working Draft (2), will grow to be the main title and subtitle, "This Other World: Projections in the Haiku Manner" in Final Draft.

No. 640 on which Wright scrawls "timelessness" is:

> The spring hills grow dim,
> Today joining other days,
> Days gone, days to come. (640)

The first line "The spring hills grow dim" is changed from "The spring hills grew faint" (emphasis added) in Earliest Draft, where the past tense turns into the present tense. In his *Haiku* Blyth cites haiku by ancient Japanese haiku poet Takai Kito (1741 – 1789) in the preface to explain how haiku is presented: "In the shop, / The paper-weights on the picture-books: / The spring wind!" (I: 11). Blyth then explains about the importance of daily present life in haiku: "When we are grasping the inexpressible meaning of these things, this is life, this is living. To do this twenty-four hours a day is the Way of Haiku. It is having life more abundantly" (I: 11). Wright changes the tense from past to present because he notices that haiku should refer to "this twenty-four hours a day," in other words, "here and now," a so-called haiku moment. The impact of "timelessness" in No. 640 is greater than spring, portraying the everlasting moment when the dim growing of spring hills is eternal. Thus seasons are less relevant than themes after Working Draft (2).

The following is scrawled "Agreement," which means a joint decision that a particular course of action should be taken. It is a logical conclusion that a puppy jointly barks at the same time when a bubble bursts:

> A bounding puppy
> Chases a blue soap bubble
> And barks when it bursts. (340)

In a similar vein, Wright writes in handwriting a theme or two on each haiku in Working Draft (2).

5th stage—Cardboard Draft and Final Draft

In early May 1960 Wright cuts out each haiku in newly typewritten Working Draft (2) and mounts them theme after theme onto twenty-one large cardboard sheets. The number and each theme are scribbled in longhand at the top of each cardboard sheet. The nineteen themes (the number of verses in the parentheses) are: 1. Command (15 verses), 2. Things (59), 3. Delicacy (40), 4. Cryptic (36), 5. Relation (33), 6. Projection (78), 7. Sensation (50), 8. Agreement (1) (58), 8. Agreement (2) (89) [two cardboard sheets for Agreement], 9. Religion (49), 10. Magic (30), 11. Illusion (25), 12. Pathos (31), 13. Departure (43), 14. Timelessness (12), 15. Personification (68), 16. Duration (48), 17. Absence (23), 18. Animal-Human (7), and 19. This Other World (22). At the end of each theme are placed three asterisks as a divider between themes. "1. Command" begins with:

> For you, O gulls,
> I order salty waters
> And this leaden sky! (2)

The "Command" haiku come first because Wright knows as a fiction writer that he should begin with imperative and impressive sentences to give a strong impression to readers. Haiku in imperative sentences are more dramatic than ones depicting ordinary scenes.

4. Cryptic (36 verses) ends with:

> Standing in spring rain,
> The hitchhiker has a stance
> That nobody trusts. (154)

In No. 154 a hitchhiker standing in rain looks cryptic and distrustful to Wright. Hitchhiking is known to travel to places by getting free rides from drivers of passing cars, beginning in the 1920s, but hence in the United States, some local governments have laws outlawing hitchhiking, on the basis of drivers' and hitchhikers' own safety. No. 154 might be written under the influence of Kerouac,[24] a Beat

---

24. Weinreich notes in her introduction: "For a new generation of poets, Kerouac ended up breaking ground at a pioneering stage of an American haiku movement" (Kerouac, Book iv). Kerouac spent sixty-three days during the summer of 1956 as a fire lookout on Desolation

Generation writer and Wright's precursor haiku poet, hitchhiked in America and wrote many books about his experience like *On the Road* (1958), which Wright has a copy of (Fabre, Books & Writers, 86).

This is Cardboard Draft, consisting of twenty large cardboard sheets with 810 verses (six doubly used verses) (oversized folders 2033-2035, Yale). Except for the small number of haiku which are dropped off, Cardboard Draft is almost the same as Final Draft, "This Other World: Projection in the Haiku Manner," upon which the printed version *Haiku: This Other World* is based.

In mid-May 1960 Wright continues to work hard, going over the cardboard sheets a good many times, and gives Cardboard Draft to the typist as he says in the letter to Sablonière: "Forgive my long delay, but I've been working night and day. I must now get all these haikus typed" (Wright to Sablonière 16 May, FPC). When he sends Cardboard Draft to the typist, Wright instructs her to leave upper half-page space at the first page to fill with the first haiku to come at the beginning of the collection. At this time Wright has not decided yet what haiku comes first. The typist then makes a fair copy of the manuscript and returns it to Wright. Since he likewise knows quite well as a fiction writer that it is half successful if the novel opens with a fine paragraph, Wright is very cautious what haiku to begin with and decides on the following haiku with due consideration to the last minute:

> I am nobody:
> A red sinking autumn sun
> Took my name away. (1)

Peak, Washington. The "Desolation Pops" manuscript (Kerouac, Book 81-104) is a collection of seventy-two haiku experiments in relating his mountain loneliness to nature.

This haiku is reminiscent of Wright's *The Outsider* (1953) written under the influence of existentialism. The protagonist Cross Damon, like the poet, suffers from namelessness, selflessness, and even loss of nationality, losing his name and identity and becoming a different person, Lionel Lane.[25] The second line is changed from "A red sinking autumn sun" in Earliest Draft to "A red sinking winter sun" in Working Draft (1) and back again to "A red sinking autumn sun." Autumn, Wright probably judges, is more appropriate than winter for those who lost their name and identity. After wavering in his judgment of what season, Wright categorizes No. 1 as "Cryptic" first and then as "Religion" in Working Draft (2). No. 1 is written along with the mind of Zen Buddhism, following Blyth's note that selflessness is one of the minds of the haiku poet: "It is a condition of selflessness in which things are seen without reference to profit or loss, even of some remote, spiritual kind" (I: 155). To realize the selflessness (non-ego), Wright might have referred to Ikkyū's[26] waka cited in Blyth's *Haiku*:

> Myself of long ago,
> In nature
> Non-existent:
> No final destination,
> Nothing of any value. Ikkyū (I: 159)

On 22 May 1960, although the themes written in longhand on the cardboard sheets seem important, Wright instructs the typist to eliminate them leaving intact the order of haiku as well as theme dividers:

> I'm now through with the haikus. You know, I cannot let anything out of my hands as long as I feel and know that there is something else to do with it. But now, for better or worse, I'm

---

25. For further details, see Kiuchi, "Zen" (34).
26. Ikkyū Sōjun (1394 – 1481) is a Japanese Zen Buddhist monk and poet who had an impact on Japanese art and literature with Zen attitudes.

giving the ms. to the typist. Maybe I'm fooling around with these tiny poems. I could not let them go. I was possessed by them. Now, soon, I shall see what the publisher says about them. There are 811 in all and they will make a ms of some 80 pages. Well, that's done. All I have to do is to proof the typing . . . Thank you for the booklet on Zen. I've not yet had time to look at it, but will do so in a day or two. (Wright to Sablonière, 22 May, FPC)

Final Draft, "This Other World: Projections in the Haiku Manner," consists of 817 haiku with 82 pages with ten haiku on each page except seven on the first page (box 70, folder 834, Yale). However, it has 816 haiku because the following is doubly used as 349 and 439:

A church bell at dusk:
The evening sun's slanting rays
Dying on my wall. (349 and 439)

Wright mistakenly pastes this haiku from Working Draft (2) twice onto Cardboard Draft for there are two categories of "Agreement" which lead to confusion.

V. The Published Version

On 8 June 1960 Wright sends Final Draft, the eighty-two page manuscript of haiku, "This Other World: Projections in the Haiku Manner," to his publisher Targ to ask for their advice as a friend and to find out their editorial reactions, reporting to Reynolds (Fabre, Quest 509; 620n24):

Listen, today I've sent to William Targ of World Publishing a ms. of poems [haiku]. Now, I did not send you this little ms. first (it runs to 80 pages) because I feel that it has no commercial value. And I don't know if you would want to handle poetry or not. The ms. was not submitted to World, but sent to Targ as my personal friend for his reaction. (Wright to Reynolds, 8 June, qtd. Fabre, Quest 620n24)

Targ nevertheless turns down the manuscript about one month later after Wright sends the manuscript to Targ: "You do have the poetic gift . . . But after reading a few hundred, a quiet monotony sets in . . . I should say that a fine little book could be produced from a careful selection; but frankly, I don't have the courage to undertake such a publication, publishable though it be" (Targ to Wright, 6 July, qtd. Rowley 515). At the bad news Wright confides to Sablonière: "I'm rather depressed, but there seems to be no specific reason" (Wright to Sablonière, 19 July, qtd. Fabre, Quest 512). Reynolds, who later receives the haiku manuscript, also writes Wright doubting that it is easy to sell the haiku (Wright to Reynolds, 21 July, FPC). However, Wright dies of a heart attack on 28 November 1960. Final Draft, "This Other World: Projections in the Haiku Manner," is thus deposited and housed at Beinecke Library at Yale University until it is published by Hakutani and Tener as *Haiku: This Other World* in 1998.

For the title of the published version, Ellen Wright decides on *Haiku: This Other World* in coorperation with Hakutani and Tener. As far as Final Draft, "This Other World: Projections in the Haiku Manner" with ten haiku in two columns on each page, is concerned, Wright intends the reader to read from the whole left column first and then to the whole right column next and so forth. The arrangement is, for example, quite clear, judging from the "Command" cardboard sheet in Cardboard Draft where fifteen haiku are arranged in one column vertically from top to bottom. However, Hakutani and Tener, editors for *Haiku: This Other World*, pick up each haiku in Final Draft side by side from the top left haiku to the next right one on the same level and then the same way on the next level from the left haiku to the right one on the same level and so forth. The published version has one column with four haiku on each page from 1 to 205 except one haiku only on page 205. Each of the haiku is numbered consecutively 1 through 817. The arrangement inconveniences in the printed version such as the order change happen: "For you, O gulls" verse (2) should be followed by "Sweep away the clouds" verse (4), not by "Keep straight down this block" verse (3). Moreover, even though Wright omitted nineteen themes, Final Draft has sixty-seven theme dividers comprising of three O's in the V shape, which are omitted in the published version by the editors. For instance, the first theme divider of three O's in Final Draft appears between "O Anvil, be beaten" verse (15), categorized as "Command," and "In a misty rain" verse (17), categorized as "Things," for the above-mentioned reason to divide into two categories "Command" and "Things." Without theme dividers the reader of the published version would not be able to know where one theme ends and changes to another.

In conclusion, Wright meets haiku through Beat poets and his interest in Zen Buddhism when he is ill after his previous encounter with Japan and Japanese culture. He continues to write twenty haiku a day for half a year. The arrangement of haiku is made in accordance with season at the suggestion of a Japanese professor. However, the arrangement is later made according to themes, which are hidden because Wright strikes them out from the cardboard sheets and does not include them in Final Draft. Although themes are hidden, theme dividers remain. It might be more helpful to analyze Wright's haiku through his hidden categorization. Wright's theme categorization would be sure to serve more for interpretation of *Haiku: This Other World*.

Works Cited

Blyth, R. H. *Haiku.* Four volumes. Tokyo: Hokuseido, 1949-1952.

Fabre, Michel. Fabre's Private Collection of Richard Wright Papers, Paris, France (FPC).

—. *Richard Wright: Books & Writers.* Jackson: UP of Mississippi, 1990.

—. *The Unfinished Quest of Richard Wright.* Urbana: U of Illinois P, 1993.

Hakutani, Yoshinobu. *Richard Wright and Haiku.* Columbia: U of Missouri P, 2014.

Harrington, Oliver. *Why I Left America and Other Essays.* Jackson: UP of Mississippi, 1993.

Hellwig, David J. "Afro-American Reactions to the Japanese and the Anti-Japanese Movement, 1906-1924." *Phylon* 38 (1) (1st Quarter 1977): 93-104.

Kearney, Reginald. "Japan: Ally in the Struggle against Racism, 1919-1927." *Contributions in Black Studies* 12 (1994): 117-28.

Kerouac, Jack. *Book of Haikus.* Ed. Regina Weinreich. New York: Penguin Books, 2003.

Kiuchi, Toru. "Zen Buddhism in Richard Wright's Haiku." *The Other World of Richard Wright.* Ed. John Zheng. Jackson: UP of Mississippi, 2011.

Kiuchi, Toru and Yoshinobu Hakutani. *Richard Wright: A Documented Chronology, 1908 – 1960.* Jefferson, NC: McFarland, 2014.

"The Pulp Magazines Project." (https://www.pulpmags.org/content/info/argosy.html)

Ray, David, and Robert M. Farnsworth, eds. *Richard Wright: Impressions and Perspectives.* Ann Arbor: U of Michigan P, 1973.

Roberts, Brian Russell, and Keith Foulcher, eds. *Indonesian Notebook: A Sourcebook on Richard Wright and the Bandung Conference.* Durham: Duke UP, 2016.

Rowley, Hazel. *Richard Wright: The Life and Times.* New York: A John Macrae Book, 2001.

Wright, Richard. *Black Boy (American Hunger).* New York: Harper Perennial, 1993.

—. *Black Power.* 1953. New York: Harper Perennial, 1995.

—. *The Color Curtain.* Cleveland: World Publishing, 1956.

—. *Haiku: This Other World.* Ed. Yoshinobu Hakutani and Robert L. Tener. New York: Arcade, 1989.

—. *Native Son.* New York: Harper & Brothers, 1940.

—. *The Outsider.* New York: Harper & Brothers, 1953.

—. Richard Wright Papers, Firestone Library, Princeton University.

—. Richard Wright Papers, James Weldon Johnson Collection, Beinecke Rare Book and Manuscript Library, Yale University.

Departing spring hesitates in the late cherry blossoms

Poet: Buson
Artist: McDonald Wright

"'To sing the haiku the american way is a beautiful thing':

The Haiku of Etheridge Knight

Tom Morgan

ABSTRACT: This essay takes up Etheridge Knight's haiku as a means to trace his "major metaphor" of prison as a form of postcolonial cross-cultural haiku poetics. Knight's haiku often focus on those that are voiceless along with the systems that work to disenfranchise them, using their experiences and conditions to engage the unequal power dynamics silently perpetuating inequality. In mapping out the explicit and implicit walls that position the hierarchies present in Knight's haiku, and connecting these to his published comments on the role and function of haiku within his own poetic imagination, we can better understand Knight's interest in re-imagining haiku as an American form that can speak to the specific conditions and context of American settler colonialism. As well, by bringing in several of Knight's previously unpublished haiku from later in his life, we can also see that his investment in haiku was a life-long endeavor. Knight imagined his haiku as a means to advocate for change and freedom, giving voice to those who existed on the margins by criticizing the hubris connected to power and privilege.

I see the traditional haiku in American poetry as much the same way as I see, say, Scottish bagpipes in american music. Unless the instrument and the communications coming through it within the prison of our american consciousness/ historical experience, and it is rooted/grounded with the NOW, within OUR BEING, it is neither valid nor valuable. So. To me, to sing the haiku the american way is a beautiful thing.

Etheridge Knight, "A Statement from Etheridge Knight"

This essay takes up Etheridge Knight's haiku as a lens to examine his poetic voice, specifically as a means to understand his interest in the connections between oral tradition[1] and poetic language,

1. While Knight makes connections between Black oral traditions and haiku traditions, I would like to be clear that I am not making a claim in this essay about haiku being an oral tradition. Rather, I am attempting to map out Knight's own beliefs on the relationship between Black oral traditions and haiku traditions in order to identify Knight's interest in re-imagining haiku as an American form. For more context on Knight's view of the relationship between Black oral traditions and haiku traditions, see "On the Oral Nature of Poetry" and "A Statement from Etheridge Knight," both of which are quoted in this essay. Similarly, in Knight's interview with Steven Tracy, he notes "I think that Black poets, along with the Beats, have brought back the oral tradition" (19). Shirley Lumpkin notes in "Etheridge Knight" (*Afro-American Poets since 1955. Vol. 41 of Dictionary of Literary Biography*. Detroit: Gale, 1985. 202-11) that Knight "was granted the Guggenheim [Fellowship in 1974] on the basis of a proposal he had made to study the oral tradition, the speech and music he had grown up with, which form the legitimate basis of black poetry, as evidenced in the work of poets like Langston Hughes, Sterling Brown, and so many others" (206). Ugo Rubeo observes in "Voice as Lifesaver: Defining the Function of Orality on Etheridge Knight's Poetry" (In *The Black Columbiad*. Eds. W. Sollors and M. Diedrich. Cambridge: Harvard UP, 1994. 275-85) that "Knight's insistent use of oral modes — and the blues in particular — as an aesthetically accomplished solution to the

as well as the relation of both to his political activism. While Knight only published forty-four haiku during his life,[2] haiku were intimately important to his developing sense of self as a poet and public figure, and they remained an important outlet for his most important thought and work throughout the course of his career. As Knight describes in a 1986 interview with Ron Price, "My major metaphor is prison" (168), and Knight's haiku readily engage his major metaphor. Knight's use of prison as a metaphor to engage the world—whether literally or figuratively—informs the postcolonial and anti-imperial poetics driving his work. His haiku focus on the disenfranchised and voiceless, examining the history of their experiences as well as the effect of that history on their subjectivity in order to engage the unequal power dynamics that silently perpetuate inequality. These concerns remained relevant to Knight late in his career, as we will see when comparing some of Knight's published haiku with his previously unpublished haiku from later in life that are housed in the Etheridge Knight Collection at Butler University. Through taking up the relationship between language and power, Knight's haiku question the cultural, racial, sexual, and economic barriers, to name but a few, that impede freedom and happiness. Knight's interest in making his haiku distinctly

---

problematic core of his poetics: his overriding concern to avoid the danger of rootlessness" (284). For further discussion regarding the role of Black oral traditions in Knight's poetry, see also Thomas C. Johnson's "Excerpts from Notes of an Oral Rhapsodist: An Introduction to the Poetry and Aesthetic of Etheridge Knight" (*The Worcester Review* 19.1-2 [1998]: 79-8).

2. This number shifts depending upon how you count particular poems and haiku. I am counting only the poems that are labeled as haiku in his work, and not shorter poems like Knight's "Memo" poems or "Evolutionary Poem No. 1" or "Evolutionary Poem No. 2," amongst others. To this number I will add the approximately 40 haiku that exist in draft form in the Etheridge Knight Collection (MSS 011) at Butler University, ten of which are being published for the first time with this essay, and several of which I will take up later in the essay.

American, to give them, as he puts it, value by grounding them "with the NOW, within OUR BEING," allows Knight to hone his poetic voice as a means of advocating change while simultaneously giving voice to those suffering at the hands of power and privilege.

In this sense, I read Knight's "major metaphor" of prison as an embodiment of postcolonial cross-cultural haiku poetics. As Michael Collins argues in "The Antipanopticon of Etheridge Knight,"

> Throughout his poetry and prose, Knight challenges frontiers, and the walls and one-way mirrors they justify, by acting as an antipanopticon surveilling United States society and justice to look into the souls not only of prisoners but also the whole tradition that locks them in. (581)

As a veteran of the Korean War who also served time in prison once he returned home, Knight was intimately aware of prison as an extension of settler colonial practices of slavery, as well as an extension of colonial rule and colonialism's "civilizing" mission towards non-whites. This tension between punishment and citizenship, between prison and freedom, highlights the organizational logic of American colonialism's need to discipline non-conforming black and brown bodies. In mapping out the explicit and implicit walls that impose the hierarchies present in Knight's haiku, and connecting these to his published comments on the role and function of haiku within his own poetic imagination, we can better understand Knight's interest in re-imagining haiku as an American form that can speak to the specific conditions and context of American settler colonialism.

"the prison of our american consciousness": Haiku and Cross-Cultural Poetics

Knight's initial exposure to haiku came via Gwendolyn Brooks during his time in prison; as Knight observes in an interview with Stephen Tracy, Brooks used to come visit me when I was in prison. [...] And she brought me books and Japanese *haiku*. Years later I asked her how come and she said, "it was because you were too wordy in your poems." And I like *haiku*. I try to use it, I try to follow the general form. I try to bring my own American consciousness to it. You know. I try to do with the *haiku* just about what Ray Charles does with country and western. (Tracy 18)

Knight's analogy between his work in the haiku and Ray Charles' adaptations of "country and western" music helps clarify the type of cultural translation that Knight invokes when he says "I try to bring my own American consciousness" to the haiku form. In taking the traditional form and grounding it in a particular cultural and historical moment, Knight argues that any theory of aesthetics must remain culturally specific to remain relevant. As in the epigraph, without the requisite cultural specificity, "traditional haiku in American poetry" are like "Scottish bagpipes in american music": "neither valid or valuable." And yet, this is not to imply that Knight merely seeks to abandon the formal definitions connected to traditional haiku. As Knight reveals to Charles Rowell,

I write haiku for two reasons. After I began to define myself as a poet, I understood that you should master your art form. [...] To me writing haiku is a good exercise. I dig and respect them because they create an image — paint a picture — so precisely. They draw pictures in very clean lines. You say what you want to say symbolically. I work with haiku a lot in my attempt to handle the language — the word. I don't see haiku as a black form, but, then, you utilize whatever modes or vehicles are available to you. (Rowell 978)

This notion of haiku as a "good exercise" with which to "master your art form" points to the importance of the haiku in regards to Knight's aesthetic vision at both ends of his artistic career; it links not only to the concision of language Brooks implied was necessary to develop as a poet, but also to the way that linguistic precision and line organization improves poetry's visual imagery. Knight's awareness of the relation between form and content connects to his ability to "handle the language — the word" with increasing force as a poet, itself part of his work to make his haiku distinctly American.

Knight's interest in haiku also stems from its association with orality and the spoken word. In "On the Oral Nature of Poetry," Knight states that "poetry is primarily oral utterance, and the end of a poem belongs in somebody's ears rather than their eyes. [...] I [...] see the written word as an extension of the spoken word, not a separate entity" (12). The focus on poetry as an "oral utterance" stems from Knight's interest in maintaining both his relevance as a poet and his connection with his audience. The "Introduction" to *Born of a Woman* (1980), Knight's third collection, makes a similar point; here Knight observes: "You'll also notice that most of my poems are about and/or for people. That's because I see the Art of Poetry as the logos ('In the beginning was the WORD') as a TRINITY: The Poet, The Poem, and The People. When the three come together, the communion, the communication, the Art happens" (xiv). Similarly, in "A Statement from Etheridge Knight," Knight identifies his interest in haiku as stemming from its oral roots:

> I really got into haiku when I learned (read/or/"heard" somewhere) that the "original" haiku poets/were in to haiku primarily as/an/oral/ being and the "written" poem as secondary — as simply an/extension of the spoken word, more or less — certainly more. (*Frogpond* 23)

The primacy of orality for the "'original' haiku poets" creates the connection that links Knight to the haiku form. Whereas the subject matter of "traditional haiku in American poetry" was akin to "Scottish bagpipes in american music," the oral roots of haiku directly relate to Knight's own oral Black aesthetic practices, creating an intuitive cultural link between Black oral traditions and Japanese oral traditions that does not correspond with the expected discrepancy in the content of "traditional haiku."

This seemingly insignificant and yet important distinction is a product of Knight's interest in developing a poetics grounded in Black vernacular culture and practice and yet also reciprocally informed by his American identity; one that can simultaneously advocate an insurrectionary postcolonial politics while identifying as American. Knight's interest in the non-Western oral aesthetic practices of haiku stems from his interest in balancing his own seemingly contradictory aesthetic practices that concurrently draw from black and white American perspectives as well as Western and non-Western cultural sources.

Thus while Knight observes in the Rowell interview that he doesn't "see haiku as a black form" and instead utilizes "whatever modes or vehicles are available" to him as a poet (978), he also points out earlier in the interview that

> I think the Black Aesthetic differs from the European Aesthetic mainly [...] because it does not separate art or aesthetics from the other levels of life. It does not separate art from politics, art from economics, art from ethics, or art from religion. Art is a functional and a commercial endeavor. The artist is not separate from the people. (Rowell 967)

The desire to maintain an explicit connection between "art" and "life," between the "artist" and the "people," points to one of Knight's foundational Black Aesthetic values. And it differs from what Knight defines here as a "European Aesthetic," and what I would further identify as a white, European-derived American aesthetic, in adhering to an oral tradition that does not separate the spoken and the written word. Thus, Knight's interest in the orality of haiku is relevant in that it supplements an absence he finds in white American poetry, even as Knight subsequently modifies the "general form" of haiku to make it better fit with his "American consciousness." It is the oral origins of the haiku that make it formally "available" to Knight via the legacy it shares with the

African American vernacular tradition in ways that, say, a white American perspective is not equally "available," even though he lays claim to an "American consciousness." For Knight, the elasticity of American identity as an identifying category is broader and more inclusive than the subordinate appellations of white and black, which, not surprisingly, corresponds to the elasticity of aesthetic theory that allows Knight to modify traditional haiku in order to make them culturally and historically relevant for an "American consciousness."

Knight's growing familiarity with poetic form and language in general, and metaphor specifically, is also connected to his initial experiences with haiku while in prison. In a 1986 interview with Ron Price, Knight asserts "My major metaphor is prison. I think art is ultimately about freedom, the celebration of that freedom — whether it's individual or general" (168). Knight's metaphor of prison refers not only to his literal incarceration, but also figuratively to the ways in which barriers are created, imposed, and maintained between different individuals and groups in society, most often as a direct manifestation of power. In *Black Voices from Prison* (1970), a collection of prison writing published after Knight was released from prison, Knight quotes a now classic observation by Malcolm X — "'Don't be shocked when I say that I was in prison. You're still in prison. That's what America means: prison'" (5) — before going on to observe "And it is all too clear that there is a direct relationship between men behind prison walls and men behind the myriad walls that permeate this society" (6). The parallelism between "prison walls" and "the myriad walls that permeate society" points to their structural similarity in maintaining the preferred fictions of American life; while one is literal and the other is figurative, they both serve to create barriers that impede interactions by curtailing individual freedom at the expense of maintaining social order and white supremacy. This was what I meant earlier when I pointed to American colonialism's compulsive need to discipline non-conforming black and brown bodies. It is also worth noting that these limitations function in unequal and asymmetrical ways; the higher your place in the social hierarchy, the easier it is to ignore and disregard the effects your behavior has upon those lower down on the ladder.

Knight further extends these comments on the relation between freedom and individual and collective behavior in his interview with Charles Rowell:

> Here we are — black people, oppressed. In this country, we are oppressed racially and sexually. Women are oppressed. Homosexuals in prison and in the larger society are oppressed. If you are black, a woman, a lesbian and you're in prison, you are oppressed four times. Black men will talk about being free, yet they'll have a woman walking four paces behind them and go "fag hunting." We cannot win our freedom at the expense of anybody. Many blacks — artists, educators, politicians, and other leaders — will say there's nothing to women's liberation or gay liberation. Or they will argue that if we have to become fascists to win our freedom, it's better for us to have oppressors in jail than for them to have us. But I don't feel that way; I don't think we can be free that way. I don't think the conditions of the world would allow us to be free at the expense of anybody else. (Rowell 977)

Here, Knight indicates the dangers that come with oppositional group thinking, specifically when adherence to such logic requires maintaining and advocating a hierarchy of oppression. As Knight observes, "Many blacks" feel compelled to promote their needs at the expense other exploited groups. And it is the open and public adherence by those in charge of the group — "politicians, and other leaders"—that serves to rationalize an exclusionary mentality. As an example of the "myriad walls that permeate society," Knight publicly separates himself from the political limitations often connected to the Black Arts Movement, embracing a broader, intersectional definition of identity that complicates oversimplified versions of power. As well, Knight's willingness to engage the role language plays in perpetuating inequality extends to his own work; as he points out in his "Introduction" to *Born of a Woman*,

> You'll notice that I have made slight changes to some of the "older" poems. A phrase altered here and there, a word added or dropped. The reason is—while reading my poems around the country, I became aware (sometimes I was *made* aware) that I was perpetuating the racism and sexism that is inherent in our language. For instance, an "English" teacher at Bucks County Community College in Pennsylvania pointed out to me, quite firmly, that the line "And we all waited and watched, like indians at a corral"—from "Hard Rock Returns"—contained a racist phrase. And she was right. And so I changed "like indians at a corral" to "like a herd of sheep." In another instance, a young woman poet at the 1975 National Poetry festival convinced me that the last lines in "The Idea of Ancestry"—"… and I have no sons/ to float in the space between"—was sexist. And so I changed "sons" to "children." The list goes on. On the surface, it might look like nitpicking, but actually it's not. The authority, the authenticity, the integrity of the poet's voice is "grounded" in the WORD as connotation, as evocation, as imagination (hence: image), and to perpetuate a lie, an evil, whether through omission or commission is to commit artistic and/or actual suicide. (xiv)

As Knight's self-criticism indicates, transforming the "prison of our american consciousness" ("Statement") requires not only an understanding of the dialogic relationship between prison and freedom, but the willingness to challenge both the personal and social linguistic structures that contribute to sanctioning inequality.

Knight's interest in metaphor is also a product of his relationship with the haiku. While metaphor is not a part of traditional haiku, Knight's interest in linking African American and Japanese oral traditions while also combining Western metaphor with traditional Japanese haiku points to his interest in creating a postcolonial poetic form that engages the specifics of American racism. In "A Statement from Etheridge Knight," Knight describes the value in working with haiku:

> From Haiku I also learned the syllabic importance of poetry: the ability to evoke (= spoken) a major metaphor containing (1) something *living*, a sense of motion (= verb) and a sense of time (= season, night, day, noon, etc.) — all *this* — juxtaposed or interwoven an old/concept poured from a new jug. Or better yet, (when one is lucky) if the major concept is juxtaposed with a minor one, and a new concept is born. (23)

This description extends Knight's vision of what it means to "sing the haiku the american way"; it not only draws upon traditional definitions of the haiku, but also revises that definition to allow Knight "to bring [his] own American consciousness to it." While Knight's reference to the relation between haiku and "major metaphor" prefaces his 1986 comment to Ron Price that "My major metaphor is prison" (168), the foundational relation between haiku and prison in Knight's work becomes clearer when this quote is linked with his later comments, specifically as it positions haiku as the form Knight uses to work out and develop his major poetic themes. Knight expands his understanding of the relation between oral tradition and metaphor in "The Oral Nature of Poetry," where he observes

> Generally speaking, a people's metaphors and figures of speech will come out of their basic economy. If somebody lives near the ocean and they fish, their language will be full of these metaphors. If people are farmers, they will employ that kind of figure of speech. Metaphors are alive. When they come into being, they are informed by the politics and the sociology and the economy of now. That's how language is. And when we try to use dead metaphors, metaphors that were relevant to Shakespeare's time, then the audience cannot get in because the metaphor is out of the audience's experience. (13-4)

Similar to Knight's interest in haiku as an oral form in "A Statement from Etheridge Knight," and to his interest in a Black Aesthetic that "does not separate art or aesthetics from the other levels of life" (Rowell 967), Knight sees metaphor as an extension of daily human life that links metaphor with all the complexity of lived experience. For Knight, "to sing the haiku the american way" requires grounding his haiku in a poetics of place that fits with the temporal and cultural space he inhabits. To miss remaking traditional haiku as his own is to miss the opportunity to engage his audience at the grounds of where they are at or where they need to be. It is also to miss the way Knight wants to use his haiku to make visible to the people the ways in which their freedom can and will be used against them by the settler colonial state for their own ends.

Knight's Postcolonial Haiku Aesthetics

To get clearer insight into Knight's haiku aesthetics, I would like to start by juxtaposing two of Knight's haiku, drawing upon something old and something new. The first haiku is the fourth in a series of nine haiku from *Poems from Prison*, published 1968 while Knight was still in prison, while the second is from "Haiku for the Homeless," a previously unpublished four haiku sequence from Knight's papers at Butler University. Explicitly or implicitly, both haiku are informed by Knight's major metaphor of prison. While the fourth haiku in *Poems from Prison* series does not directly address prison, several of the other haiku in the series do. When coupled with the title of the collection itself, which identifies the place from which this work arises, Knight's subject matter creates a combination of implicit and explicit markers regarding his major metaphor:

> 4
> To write a blues song
> is to regiment riots
> and pluck gems from graves. (18)

This haiku is a complex two-part metaphor; the initial source of the metaphor is "To write a blues song," which is then connected to two targets: "to regiment riots/ and pluck gems from graves." Each part contains both a verb and a noun; it is not merely the identification between nouns that creates the metaphor, but rather the play between the action of the verbs. Thus, the metaphor focuses not on linking "blues song," "riots," and "gems from graves," but on identifying the connections between writing, regimenting, and plucking these objects. Both targets focus on using the past in a productive manner from the perspective of the present, not only to learn from that past but also to move beyond the problems created and embodied in that past. It is the writing of "a blues song" that brings understanding to the chaos of "riots" and finds the value in the "gems from graves."

Each target has an interesting corollary elsewhere in Knight's own personal life. To "regiment riots" links to a quote by Martin Luther King, Jr. that Gwendolyn Brooks uses as an epigraph for her poem, "Riot," which is "A riot is the language of the unheard." While this is its own metaphor, conceptualizing a riot as a literal statement made by the disenfranchised is similar to Knight's in that both focus on understanding that should come from the event rather than dismissing the actions as irrelevant. To "pluck gems from graves" links to a line from Knight's "Hard Rock Returns to Prison from the Hospital for the Criminal Insane" in *Born of a Woman*, where a prisoner recounts "And then the jewel of a myth that Hard Rock had once bit/A screw on the thumb and poisoned him with syphilitic spit." "Jewel" functions in the same way as "gem," where value is found in past actions that make life worth living or can be used to sustain a community in times of need. The "myth" that can help sustain prisoners finds a corollary in the longer memory implied by "graves," pointing to the way that the past, even when appearing dead, still maintains value and relevance by continuing to inspire those in the present.

The second haiku, the final of four in "Haiku for the Homeless,"[3] foregrounds the interdependent relationship between people at the heart of society. As such, it is a much more figurative invocation of Knight's major metaphor of prison, one that incorporates gender along with class in articulating the walls that separate across subject position:

> 4
> My sister's sorrow
> Shouts: Shame! Shame! Shame! My sister's
> Eyes moan: Blame! Blame! Blame!

This haiku juxtaposes "My sister's sorrow" with "My sister's/ Eyes." While there is an implied speaker observing this woman, the haiku blurs the woman's experiential and man's observational perspectives in the poem by leaving the source of both the "Shame!" and "Blame!" unspoken. The relationship between the two is also left purposefully ambiguous. On the one hand, the use of the possessive pronoun "My" indicates an explicit connection, one that is further built by describing her as the speaker's "sister." Whether intended to convey a familial or racial connection, "sister" links the two subjects together. On the other hand, the title of the sequence, "Haiku for the Homeless," indicates a potential separation between the two, be it along class lines, gender lines, or both. This duality is consistently mirrored in almost every aspect of the poem: we do not know, for example, if her "sorrow/ Shouts" because it is manifesting itself in a confrontational manner towards the speaker, or if it instead "Shouts" because the tragic image this "sorrow" reflects calls out to the speaker even though the woman herself is silent and invisible. As well, the "Blame!" functions in a similar manner: the visuality implied by the woman's "Eyes" could castigate the speaker for observing her and doing nothing to alleviate her suffering, or the "moan" her eyes manifest could

---

3. For the full sequence of "Haiku for the Homeless," see the accompanying "Ten Unpublished Haiku by Etheridge Knight."

be one that blames herself for her own predicament. In a very real sense, these possibilities function simultaneously, and the dialogic relationship between the two perspectives highlights both the actual connections they should share as people while also indicating the barriers that currently exist between their different subject positions.

Several of Knight's other published haiku extend — either implicitly or explicitly — his examination of both prison and the barriers existing between people. Haiku six from the nine haiku series in *Poems from Prison* reads:

> 6
> The falling snow flakes
> Can not blunt the hard aches nor
> Match the steel stillness. (19)

In presenting the relationship between man and nature, the impact of nature on humanity is less than the impact created by incarceration, and the usual quiet silence invoked by winter and snowfall pales in comparison to the "hard aches" and "steel stillness" of imprisonment. Similarly, the normative seasonal allusion of winter as one of ending or death is refigured as calming: because snow is less powerful and cannot protect inmates from the harms that awaits them in prison, death is preferable to the experiences they will undergo in prison. Another haiku from a four haiku series in *Belly Songs and Other Poems* begins

> 1
> Outside, the thunder
> Shakes the prison walls; inside
> My heart shakes my ears. (24)

The outside/inside dichotomy in this haiku draws a relationship between the outside world and internal subjectivity, connecting the natural imagery of "thunder" and "heart" with the barriers of "prison walls" and "ears." While ears would traditionally invoke the natural, the comparison with prison walls points to the way that, from an auditory perspective, fear and emotional reactions impact how we engage the world, and can impede us from acting otherwise.[4] Finally, there is "The Penal Farm," a haiku from "Indiana Haiku — 2" in *Born of a Woman*:

> The wire fence is tall.
> The lights in the prison barracks
> Flick off, one by one.

The cutting word of "tall" marks the two parts of this haiku, leaving it up to readers to determine how to connect the halves. Read neutrally, there is a fence enclosing the space, and night time comes as the barracks slowly go dark. Reading this through Knight's major metaphor, however, offers a much starker message. It is the height of the wire fence that signifies its power, one that leads to the reciprocal consequences for prisoners: the lights "flick[ing] off" is a euphemism for the death of the subjectivity and intellect of the prisoners as one by one they succumb to the conditions of their incarceration. The second reading becomes even more compelling when we also recognize that there is no marker for night time in the poem, and that the autonomy and agency of deciding when to turn off their lights would be something already withheld from prisoners, especially on a work farm.

Knight's unpublished haiku are similarly vested in engaging the systemic inequity of contemporary American society. In a haiku

---

4. I would read this ear as an inner ear, much the same as Ralph Ellison describes the inner eye in Invisible Man: "Nor is my invisibility exactly a matter of a biochemical accident to my epidermis. That invisibility to which I refer occurs because of a peculiar disposition of the eyes of those with whom I come into contact. A matter of the construction of their inner eyes, those eyes with which they look through their physical eyes upon reality" (3).

dated June 1984 and written in Eagleville, PA, Knight describes the building of a prison as an affront to the natural world:

> Right over there men
> Assault the trees and earth to
> Build a prison-damn!

The intentional violence identified by "assault" positions the ongoing work of these men as a form of sustained hostility towards nature as well as the future inmates that will be housed in this prison. While "damn!" functions to round the syllable count of the line, it also renders a judgment on the work being described. This haiku also connects with and anticipates haiku 6 from *Poems from Prison*. Here, the violence to the land is literal and stark, while violence in that haiku is psychic in undermining the impact of seasonal imagery. Connecting these two haiku offers a way to better understand Knight's critique of Western colonial notions of ownership and objectification of the land as ongoing and cumulative. Another unpublished haiku from November 1988 engages the more personal dynamic of sexual violence

> This morning Billy
> Could not meet my eyes. Last night
> Hank had licked his thighs.

The haiku is set in Ft. Washington Shelter rather than in prison, but Hank's assault creates a dynamic that not only leaves Billy's subjectivity and sense of self changed, but positions the narrative voice as witness without clear recourse to engage the problem. Much like the final haiku from "Haiku for the Homeless" above, the focus is on making visible the most oftentimes invisible unequal structural relationships that exist between different subject positions when engaging the various power dynamics coming into the encounter, which I would identify here as the barriers that have been put up between Billy and the narrator by the actions of Hank.

The seven haiku discussed here are not the only ones engaging Knight's major metaphor of prison, along with the limitations enacted upon subjectivity by power, violence, and dominance.

One new aspect found in the unpublished haiku is Knight's direct critique of Ronald Reagan, the 40th President of the United States from 1981-1989. While neither of the two haiku included here are particularly compelling in and of themselves, they are interesting in that they offer an extension into the institutional and organizational dynamics of Knight's prison metaphor. While there are prison guards and racists along with those perpetuating inequality and celebrating national holidays (see the Fourth of July haiku published here for the first time as one example), as well as those adversely impacted by U. S. imperialism in Knight's other haiku, those who organize and run the system have not been made visible. Reagan becomes a particularly apt figure in this sense for a couple of different reasons. First, there is the allure of power that those in Reagan's position represent. As presented in this first haiku, Reagan's virility and masculinity in performing his office is sexually arousing to his wife — she climaxes with no physical contact besides him "lick[ing] his lips":

> Reagan ripped her check
> To buy guns + bombs; he licks his lips,
> And Nancy cums!

His attractiveness is based upon both the violence of his actions — "ripped" — and the potential violence of his purchase — "guns + bombs" — decisions that would sustain the action and violence seen in previous haiku. It also functions as an opposite to the haiku on sexual violence, although the interest in violence that creates consensual attraction between man and wife is itself problematic here. The second haiku, "On Ronald Robert Reagan (666#)," invokes the longstanding view of Reagan as the

Antichrist in the title[5] before turning to the community Reagan most harmed during his presidency and allowing a member of that community to describe the type of white privilege Reagan represents:

> Black grandmother speaks:
> "White man say deep truth 3 ways:
> Angry, drunk, joking!"

That none of the three types of "deep truth" are based upon an honest or authentic engagement with others points to the power vested in white male subjectivity, specifically when engaging Blacks, and even further, Black women. The generational knowledge carried here also positions the legacy of white supremacy as an established and ongoing problem.

The choice to engage the imperialist and structural aspect of his prison metaphor helps bring Knight's vision of an American haiku poetics full circle. If, as Knight claims, "art is ultimately about

5. The belief in Reagan as the Antichrist is based upon a passage from the Book of Revelation combined with the fact that Ronald Wilson Reagan's three names (first, middle, and last) each have six letters, making him 666. Reagan's particularly harmful long-term impact upon African American communities, including the introduction of crack cocaine via Iran-Contra and the massive growth of the prison industrial complex, makes him a hated figure for many African Americans, from Knight's time to today. See, for example, Killer Mike's 2012 "Reagan," which is critical of Reagan's involvement in drug trafficking in Black neighborhoods as well as for lying about Iran-Contra and selling "arms for hostages." The song samples Reagan's public denials regarding Iran-Contra, and the song ends with

> I leave you with four words: I'm glad Reagan dead
> Ronald Wilson Reagan
> Ronald Wilson Reagan
> Ronald (6) Wilson (6) Reagan (6)
> Ronald (6) Wilson (6) Reagan (666).

freedom" (Price 168), then Knight's haiku challenge us to engage that freedom through leaning in and learning to understand the difficulties others experience. Whether implicitly or explicitly, individually or collectively, Knight's fusion of form foregrounds a postcolonial praxis for his American haiku that champions the voice of the people. In doing so he challenges the institutionalized white supremacy of Western colonial thought, one that promotes the logic of incarceration his major metaphor seeks to undo. In recognizing that breaking down the barriers that exist between people is the key to transforming our social order, Knight challenges his readers to stand up to silence and indifference.

Ten Unpublished Haiku by Etheridge Knight[6]

This is a sampling of the forty-plus unpublished haiku that are a part of the Etheridge Knight Collection (MSS 011) at Butler University. Butler's collection is made up of the materials in Knight's possession when he died, mostly from 1982-1991. The bulk of Knight's manuscripts and papers are housed in the Ward M. Canaday Center at the University of Toledo; there is also a Knight collection at the Indiana Historical Society.

The subject matter of these ten haiku correspond to similar themes in Knight's other 44 published haiku along with his poetry in general: prison, sexuality, politics, violence, identity, and nature.

---

6. The location for each of the ten haiku in the Etheridge Knight Collection (MSS 011) is as follows:

Haiku 1-4 are in Box 1, folder 7
Haiku 5 is in Box 1, folder 4
Haiku 6 is in Box 1, folder 4
Haiku 7 is in Box 1, folder 5
Haiku 8 is in Box 1, folder 5
Haiku 9 is in Box 1, folder 5
Haiku 10 is in Box 1, folder 7

"Haiku for the Homeless" is similar to other haiku series in Knight's work, most notably the nine haiku series "Haiku," first published in *Poems from Prison* (1968). As well, prison is a primary touchpoint for Knight throughout his career; as Knight noted in a 1986 interview with Ron Price, "My major metaphor is prison" (168).

The specificity of the haiku directed at Reagan is new but not completely surprising. There are letters in the Butler collection discussing Reagan's second inauguration and the need to speak out against his ongoing policies: "I think it'd be a good time for all of us to get together and say our say: so soon after ol 'triple-six's' inauguration." Knight also asserts that "[we] got to change this rhythm in Reagan's dance."[7]

Finally, governmental and military violence, along with the role that state-sanctioned violence plays in the socialization of youth and the celebration of American life and identity in general, also come up in several other of Knight's already published haiku.

---

7. Both quotes are from a letter dated March 23, 1985 that can be found in Box 2, folder 11.

Haiku for the Homeless[8]

1.
I see her alone
Begging quarters from strangers:
A fallen angel

2.
X-mas crowds patter
Winter's winds tear her beggar's bag
"Happy Hanukah"

---

8. "Haiku for the Homeless" is a four haiku sequence that exists in two different versions in the Etheridge Knight Collection. The second version can be found in Box 1, folder 2, and reads

Haiku for the Homeless

[at top]
Sister of mine
See you in the flat shadows
An angel fallen

1.
X-mas crowds patter past
Red and green lights blink and blink
"Happy Hannukah"

2.
Match Christian cheers
Winter's wind tears her beggar's bag
Alone in the drone

3.
My sister's sorrow
Groans: Shame! Shame! Shame! My sister's
Eyes moan: Blame! Blame! Blame!

3.
Match the Christian cheers
Red and green lights blink and blink[9]
Alone in the drone

4.
My sister's sorrow
Shouts: Shame! Shame! Shame! My sister's
Eyes moan: Blame! Blame! Blame!

Right over there men
Assault the trees and earth to
Build a prison-damn!
                    EK
                    Eagleville, PA
                    June, 1984[10]

Haiku

This morning Billy
Could not meet my eyes. Last night
Hank had licked his thighs.
                    Nov. 1988
                    Ft. Washington Shelter

---

9. This line has a connection to one of the Indiana Haiku from *Born of a Woman* (98):

    Indiana Avenue 1949
    Neons flash red and green.
    April rains on still street, Man
    Nods, Red lights blink, blink.

10. A second version of this haiku also exists in the collection and can be found in Box 1, folder 5:

    Beyonf this green field,   [misspelling in the original]
    Men assault the earth, trees,
    Building a prison — damn!

90

Reagan ripped her check
To buy guns + bombs; he licks his lips,
And Nancy cums!

Fourth of July!
Barbeque…beer…flags…cheer…
Tomorrow war…blood…open graves[11]

On Ronald Robert Reagan
   (666#)

Black grandmother speaks:
"White man say deep truth 3 ways:
Angry, drunk, joking!"

O praying mantis!
Facing me, kneeling! Why?
I hold no dominion

---

11. This haiku's engagement with the military, celebration, violence, and death is similar in theme to a couple of haiku in Born of a Woman, including one from Indiana Haiku—2 (42):

   Indianapolis War Memorial
   Young boys play in pairs,
   Touch the War weapons: tanks, guns,
   Dreaming blood and Death.

We also see the same theme in this haiku from Missouri Haiku (97):

   Mizzu
   R. O. T. C. March:
   Drums roll and die. White blossoms
   Float in Summer air.

I would like to thank Janice J. Knight-Mooney, Executor of Etheridge Knight's Estate, for permission to publish these haiku, and Dr. Sally Childs-Helton, Head of Special Collections, Rare Books, and University Archives, for assistance in accessing the Etheridge Knight Collection (MSS 011) at Butler University, along with her willingness to work with me in during the final preparation of this essay.

Works Cited

Collins, Michael. "The Antipanopticon of Etheridge Knight." *PMLA* 123.3 (2008): 580-597. Print.

Collins, Michael. *Understanding Etheridge Knight*. Columbia: U of South Carolina P, 2012. Print.

Etheridge Knight Collection, MSS 011, Special Collections and Rare Books, Irwin Library, Butler University.

Ellison, Ralph. *Invisible Man*. New York: Vintage, 1995. Print.

Guide to the Etheridge Knight Collection, Special Collections and Rare Books, Irwin Library, Butler University.

Killer Mike. "Reagan." *R.A.P. Music*, Williams Street, 2012.

Knight, Etheridge. *Belly Songs and Other Poems*. Detroit: Broadside Press, 1973. Print.

—. *Black Voices from Prison*. New York: Pathfinder Press, 1970. Print.

—. *Born of a Woman*. Boston: Houghton Mifflin Company, 1980. Print.

—. *The Essential Etheridge Knight*. Pittsburgh: U of Pittsburgh P, 1986. Print.

—. "Letters." *Callaloo* 19.4 (1996): 956-964. Print.

—. "On the Oral Nature of Poetry." *Painted Bride Quarterly* 32/33 (1988): 12-6.

—. *Poems From Prison*. Detroit: Broadside, 1968. Print.

*Knight, Etheridge. "A Statement from Etheridge Knight." *Frogpond* 1982.

Price, Ron. "The Physicality of Poetry: An Interview with Etheridge Knight." *New Letters: A Magazine of Fine Writing* 52.2-3 (Winter-Spring 1986): 167-176. Print.

Rowell, Charles H. "An Interview with Etheridge Knight." *Callaloo* 19.4 (1996): 967-980. Print.

Tracy, Steven C. and Etheridge Knight. "A MELUS Interview." *MELUS* 12.2 (Summer 1985): 7-23. Print.

moonshine
few drops go a long way
Up!

Poet: Franjo Ordanić
Artist: Sandra Šamec

JUXTAPOSITIONS SPECIAL SECTION

Haiga From
The Haiku Foundation
Galleries

A new selection of haiga from the Haiga Galleries shows a great deal of variety, demonstrating how the field is opening up to different forms of visual expression in the Western world. Some of the defining characteristics of haiku, such the compactness, the use of suggestion rather than definition, and the sense of the rhythm of the visual and vocal language are present in the best of these haiga as well, from whatever country. A few comparisons with traditional Japanese haiga may give us some idea of how the field of haiga is evolving here in the West.

In term of composition, we can see that for us the total space is generally more filled than in Japanese haiga, which is not surprising since the same is true comparing Western with Japanese traditional paintings. Another significant comparison is with the media chosen for haiga. While Japanese works usually make use of ink, brush and paper (the same tools that have been used for writing until the computer age), Western haiga poets most often choose photography, with the poem printed rather than handwritten. Although this adds clarity to the images, it sacrifices some of the individual characteristics that appear in brush painting and handwriting. It may be that as time goes on, more Westerners will try their hand with just brush and ink, perhaps with a little color.

We can keep in mind that in haiga, the skill of the artist is not the most important factor. In Japan, for example, the poet Issa was technically a terrible painter, at best like a real beginner, yet his paintings have an inner resonance that make them very special and appealing. I doubt there is any haiku poet, East or West, who couldn't paint as well as Issa, and this should give us all courage. The use of photography and computer graphics certainly adds to the range of work as we can see in this grouping, but we should not give up the simplicity and direct expression of hand-drawn and handwritten haiga. With that caveat, the group of haiga here covers a wide range of observations and feelings, including some delightful surprises. Enjoy, and try it yourself!

— Steve Addiss

Haiga: "but"

but
through the mist
apricot blossoms

Poet/Artist: Stephen Addiss

but

through

the

mist

apricot

blossoms

Haiga: "Solstice 1986"

solstice

Poet/Artist: Marlene Mountain

Haiga: "tired of this world"

tired of this world . . .
suddenly moonlight
through my window

Poet/Artist: Ron C Moss

tired of this world...
suddenly moonlight
through my window

Haiga: "paper blown in"

paper blown in
caught in branches,
  creased by rain
origami flowers

Poet/Artist: Ellen Peckham

Haiga: "expanding universe"

expanding universe
the smallness of a pebble
in the zen garden

Poet/Artist: Pamela A. Babusci

expanding
universe
the
smallness
of
a
pebble
in
the
zen
garden

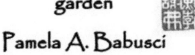

Pamela A. Babusci

Haiga: "tango"

tango
I dance to the tune
on the warm sun spots

Poet/Artist: Lidia Rozmus

tango
I dance to the tune
on the warm sun spots

Haiga: "cement carts"

the basin of her eyes
were cement carts
from cloud cover

Poet/Artist: Guy Beining

THE BASIN OF HER EYES WERE CEMENT CASTS FROM CLOUD COVER

Clouds widen the sharper context of lungs   He carried his BAG as if it were a cloud.

Haiga: "the snail"

a face
like everyone else's . . .
the snail

Poet: Issa
Artist: Jessica Tremblay

Old Pond Comics

Jessica Tremblay

a face
like everyone else's...
the snail

Kobayashi Issa

Tr. David G. Lanoue haikuguy.com/issa

www.oldpondcomics.com

Haiga: "spider silk"

spider silk—
the dreams
that came true

Poet/Artist: Beth McFarland

spider
silk –

the dreams
that came true

Haiga: "game of catch"

a game of catch
the dog turns his head
back and forth

Poet/Artist: Cor van den Heuvel

a game of catch
the dog turns his head
back and forth

Haiga: "magnolia"

magnolia in bloom
stopped for a moment
the melody in my head

Poet/Artist: Maria Tomczak

magnolia in bloom
stopped for a moment
the melody in my head

Haiga: "rhythm"

silence stilling the lingering rhythm

Poet/Artist: Paul Geiger

silence stilling the lingering rhythms

Haiga: "winter"

winter
only my late mother
called me Johnny

Poet/Artist: John Levy

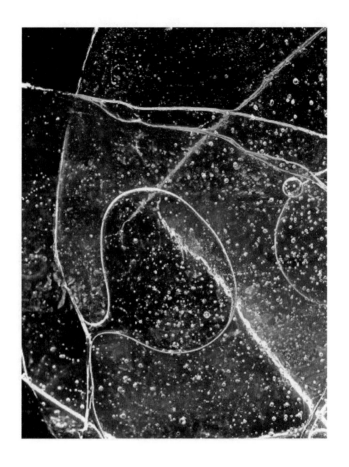

winter

only my late mother

called me Johnny

Haiga: "late autumn"

late autumn
the stand of reeds
when everyone's gone

Poet/Artist: Sandi Pray

late autumn
    the sound of reeds
        when everyone's gone

Haiga: "the studio"

in the studio
frost flowers on the windows
drinking hot wine

Poet/Artist: Geert Verbeke

in the studio
frost flowers on the windows
drinking hot wine

Haiga: "distance"

distance
and now
what

Poet/Artist: Jean LeBlanc

Haiga: "in the eyes"

in the eyes
the horizon
in silence

Poet/Artist: Toni Piccini

IN THE EYES

THE HORIZON

IN SILENCE

Haiga: "wind"

out to pasture
only the wind upon
her bent back

Poet/Artist: Debbie Strange

out to pasture

only the wind upon

her bent back

words/ image©D.Strange

Haiga: "sleepwalking"

sleepwalking
through the clockwork
of cicadas

Poet: Wolfgang Beutke
Artist: Anne-Dore Beutke

Sleepwalking
through the clockwork
of cicadas

Haiga: "first time"

first time
meeting the family
he brings his dog

Poet: Beth McFarland
Artist: anonymous woodcut

Haiga: "gulls"

voiceless gulls —
the sky resonates
flapping wings

Poet/Artist: Richard Goldberg

voiceless gulls--
the sky resonates
flapping wings

Haiga: "ladybug"

sowing snap peas
on my hand
a ladybug

Poet: Corine Timmer
Artist: pixelbay

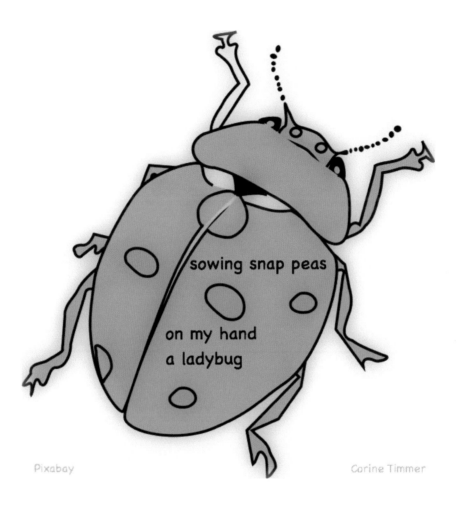

sowing snap peas

on my hand
a ladybug

Corine Timmer

Haiku of the North:

A Review of *Haiku in Canada: History, Poetry, Memoir.*

David Grayson

Carter, Terry Ann. *Haiku in Canada: History, Poetry, Memoir.* Victoria, British Columbia. Ekstasis Editions. 2020. Softcover. 214 pages. ISBN: 978-1-77171-382-5.

The corpus of English-language haiku literature encompasses histories of haiku of specific countries, biographies of classic and contemporary poets of different nationalities, as well as a bevy of country and regional anthologies. Terry Ann Carter's new book, *Haiku in Canada: History, Poetry, Memoir*, is a different animal.

At first glance, the table of contents reads like a standard history text. Initial chapters tell the stories of "Early Pioneers" and the Haiku Society of Canada. A later chapter features over a dozen regional groups. It's only the final chapter title in the list, "My Life in Haiku," that gives a hint of what else is inside.

The subtitle *History, Poetry, Memoir* reflects the combination of genres that comprise the work: historical writing, poetry, anecdote, memoir, and even historiography. Eschewing an exclusive historical narrative approach, Carter's model was *The Pillow Book* by the Heian Court writer Sei Shōnagon, which included "essays, anecdotes, poems, opinions, interesting events in court, and her famous lists."

A mixed-format approach can be risky. Foregoing the reliable benefits of a purely historical study (or memoir or anthology) requires offering the reader something else. Fortunately, *Haiku in Canada* does not suffer in comparison. In fact, the varied approach is a strength. The layers of other writing — the author's personal stories, contributions from other figures, and a hearty sampling of poetry — provides both helpful context and gives flesh to the events and the art.

After an obligatory primer about haiku for unfamiliar readers, the first topic covered is the haiku produced in the internment camps in the Second World War. The author notes that meeting Susumu Tabata, a Japanese-Canadian poet who was imprisoned in a camp, "opened the door for more research on other camps and other writing." She writes that "haiku circles were formed to help normalize the conditions of extremity," as in this poem from the diary of Kaoru Ikeda:

> picking berries
> I happen on a bear print
> in the Slocan mountains

Just as Carter allows haiku to bear some of the weight of history telling, she also grants the participants in the history to speak to the reader directly. One humorous instance is Toronto poet Chris Faiers' account of his first meeting with prominent haiku poets in the 1970s:

> "I suspect that most of us who met that evening at Eric's [Eric Amann] condo were initially apprehensive about meeting other Canadaian haiku poets. I didn't know if it would be a snooty

gathering of multilingual academics, or Zen practitioners, or Japanophiles, expat Japanese, or what! So it was comfortable to look around Eric's crowded little living room and learn that we were all pretty darn normal Canadians."

Details like this are particularly effective at bringing history to life. The reader can feel like they are in Amann's "little living room" breathing and discussing haiku.

Complementing the richness of the first-hand accounts is the comprehensive historical coverage, which reflects the author's trove of primary source material. In the "Fore/word," she references her "collection of papers, newsletters, journals, emails, personal notes, letters, books, chapbooks — all pointing to the development of haiku in Canada."

There are bios of poets that are household names to global haiku readers, from André Duhaime to Dorothy Howard to George Swede (and lesser known ones as well). But in important ways, the heart of the book may be the chapter entitled "Regional Groups of Haiku Canada." As the name implies, every group associated with Haiku Canada is portrayed. A few profiles are quite brief; for example, the Sudbury (Ontario) entry is less than a page. But it is these local communities — some older and more storied, others small or recently established — that comprise what Canadian haiku is all about. They convey the reach of haiku forums across the nation. I was pleasantly surprised to learn that there is an active community in Whitehorse, the small capital of Yukon Territory (the group hosted the Haiku Canada conference in 2016). Pairing acclaimed poets with the breadth of local entities gives a fuller picture of Canadian haiku.

In the section devoted to British Columbia, Carter discusses the activities that include poets from Washington state and Haiku Northwest (a member group of the Haiku Society of America). This makes sense as borders are porous (especially in the digital age) and there is ongoing exchange. One area where further inquiry might have borne fruit is the larger relationship between the Canadian and US haiku communities. Canadians have served in notable roles in US haiku organizations and journals. Has this drawn energy away from Canadian institutional work or has it fed it?

Following the coverage of organizations is a chapter devoted to haiku in French Canada. It's interesting to learn about the early challenges faced by French-language writers. As late as 1985, editor Francine Chicoine noted that "French Canada had no haiku society, magazines or anthologies" but over time grew and thrived "on a continent where English predominates." But there's no mention of the political climate between French and English speakers and if any of these tensions intruded into the world of haiku.

As the reader learns from the first pages, the author is a devoted family member of Canadian haiku. In this way, the final two chapters, which fill out the backdrop of Carter's involvement, are a fitting coda. The last chapter, "My Life in Haiku," is a mirror of the larger book, a miscellany.

A reference like *Haiku in Canada* is valuable in several ways. First, it can function as a springboard for further scholarship, whether it be unearthing more about the internment camps or the haiku of indigenous writers. Second, it can serve as a trusted reference for the wider history of poetry in Canada, of which haiku is one stream.

Finally, and maybe most important, it can contribute to the growth of the community that it is documenting. One can imagine an individual poet in the future being inspired to start a group in their local area after learning about all of the thriving groups that are scattered across the map. A work that can become part of the community in this way is one which will stand the test of time.

On Their Roads:

A Review of
Jack Kerouac and the Traditions
of Classic and Modern Haiku

TIM SHANER

Hakutani, Yoshinobu. *Jack Kerouac and the Traditions of Classic and Modern Haiku*. New York: Lexington Books, 2019. 222 pages, hard cover. ISBN 978-1498558273.

Yoshinobu Hakutani's *Jack Kerouac and the Traditions of Classic and Modern Haiku* should appeal both to the common reader and to scholars of haiku, the Beats, and Buddhism. It is an excellent introduction to classic and modern haiku, as the title indicates, but what is most noteworthy is its thesis about the genre's influence on Jack Kerouac's work—his poetry as well as prose—and the Beat movement at large. Not only do we learn that Kerouac was a leading practitioner of haiku, grasping the philosophy behind the form in a way few did at the time (according to Allen Ginsberg), but that haiku's connection to Confucianism, Buddhism, and Zen philosophy was central to Kerouac's spiritual journey as a writer, evident in his autobiographical novels *On the Road* and of course *Dharma Bums*. In Buddhism, Kerouac found what was missing from his Catholic upbringing, such as its connection to nature — "that there is no clear-cut distinction between humans and nonhuman" (20) — its rejection of materialism and the ego, its acceptance of death as central to life's transcendental cycle of transmigration, and its embrace of a spontaneity grounded in everyday life.

Hakutani traces Kerouac's interest in Eastern philosophies back to his days at Columbia University where, with his friends Ginsberg and William Burroughs, he studied the American transcendentalists, Emerson, Thoreau, and Whitman: "Kerouac was influenced by Emerson's concept of self-reliance as he learned of Whitman's singular, stubborn independence and refusal to subscribe to society's materialistic, commercial demands." But it was from Thoreau's *Walden* and "Civil Disobedience" that Kerouac was "introduced . . . to Confucianism and Buddhism." (xv)

Hakutani notes that Kerouac was particularly drawn to "Mahayana Buddhism [which] served to change the state of defeat in the world that the Beat movement represented to the beatific acceptance of life the Buddhist texts described." Kerouac was also inspired by Confucianism's concept of *mu*, or nothingness, which is less about the existential void and more about distancing the ego from one's everyday thoughts and actions and achieving enlightenment. Interest in haiku was high in the post-war period, thanks to Harold G. Henderson's *An Introduction to Haiku: an Anthology of Poems and Poets from Basho to Shiki* (1958) and R.H. Blyth four volumes of *Haiku* (beginning in 1961). Both Ginsberg as well as Gary Snyder read from these works and were writing haiku at the time of the famous Gallery Six reading, when Ginsberg shocked the world with his reading of *Howl*.

Hakutani cites numerous passages from *On the Road* and *Dharma Bums* where, respectively, the three writers discuss Buddhist teachings. But it's not only in these texts' content that we find the influence of Buddhist philosophy as practiced in their writing of haiku, but, perhaps more interestingly, in the the the form of Kerouac's prose. Kerouac drew from his close reading of haiku masters like Bashō, Buson, and Issa an appreciation of the Zen "principle of simplicity and naturalness" (xix), of resisting the impulse toward cleverness, which we find in Kerouac's approach toward the sentence, however improvised and rambling his sentences may have been. Likewise, his cavalier stance toward revision, most notably embodied in Kerouac's composing of *On the Road* on what he called "the scroll," a 120-foot roll of paper inserted into his typewriter, stemmed from the Buddhist valorization of spontaneity, of "liberat[ing] self from the habitual way of life" and domesticated ways of thinking and living (92).

Of course, Kerouac also found this principle at work in jazz, which Hakutani addresses less in his writings on Kerouac and more in his chapter on Richard Wright, Sonia Sanchez, and James Emmanuel. I found this chapter as compelling as any in this book, particularly Hakutani's focus on Emmanuel, a poet whose work I was unfamiliar with before and hence, for me, a delightful discovery. Perhaps my fondness for the chapter is due to the fact that Buddhist philosophy is less prevalent in these writers' haiku, due to the social milieu so strongly present in these black writers' work. Since Buddhism entails a distancing from worldly matters, the latter in my mind often gets short shrift in Hakutani's readings in favor of his focus on the poetry's transcendental features. This does not mean that the author fails to address them. In his discussion of Emmanuel's *Jazz from the Haiku King* (1999), he acknowledges the poet's unique contribution to haiku: "Adding rhyme to haiku, much like deleting seasonal reference, is an innovation Emmanuel has made in his haiku" (91). His haiku also differs from traditional haiku's emphasis on individualism and selfreliance by celebrating "cooperation and dialogue" in order to fight racism and construct a new world (91): Emmanuel's jazz haiku "pounds away the door of racism. Jazz is ammunition to destroy barbarism: people will 'fall, rise hypnotized, / maybe civilized.' Through its impressionist pipe, jazz creates 'brightsoapbubbling air,' a colorful, exciting new world" (92). Still, Hakutani brings Emmanuel's haiku back in line with what jazz shares with Zen, which "teaches its followers to liberate themselves from human laws, rules, and authorities."

This leads me to my main critique of the book, which is that the author's theoretical framework—his critical investment in Buddhism—sometimes results in reductive readings, sidestepping not only instances of social critique but also alternative ways of reading the poems and prose passages. Take, for instance, his reading of the following excerpt from *On the Road* when the character Dean Moriarty (Neil Cassady) says to Sal (Kerouac), "'What's your road, man?—holyboy road, madman road, rainbow road, guppy road, any road. It's an anywhere road for anybody anyhow. Where body how?'" (125). According to Hakutani, "Dean's listing of 'holyboy road' at the top of the various roads suggests that Kerouac will succeed in his spiritual quest because he has strong faith in God." Prioritizing "holyboy" because it appears first in his list, while at the same time ignoring the other "roads," including the two sentences that follow, misses, I think, the democratic spirit of the multitude suggested by the list's final "any road," which becomes an "anywhere road for anybody anyhow." Here, we might say that the Buddhist philosophy that so engaged Kerouac served less as a singular religious pursuit and more in pragmatic terms wherein the poet, like the jazz artist, cobbles together whatever materials are at hand to construct his path in life.

On a more technical level, I think that the book could have used more editing, particularly when it comes to the last four chapters on Kerouac, which could have easily been condensed into one. While each chapter's focus is warranted—focusing first on Kerouac's understanding of classic haiku, then on Beat poetics, and finally on, respectively, *On the Road* and *Dharma Bums* — dividing them into four separate chapters results in quite a bit of overlap, with the author repeating information covered in the previous chapters. This holds true for the other chapters in the book, as well, where terms like *mu* are defined over and over again. A certain amount of repetition is understandable, since readers unfamiliar with Eastern philosophy need to be reminded from time to time of its key concepts, but when reading the book straight through, one feels compelled to skim through such moments as a result. It made sense to include such information in these chapters' original form, when they were published separately as journal articles. It also makes sense to keep such overlap in the chapters when considering the book's academic audience, since professors are more likely to assign excerpts from the book rather than the book in its entirety. But in terms of its "book feel," this narrative flaw was hard to get around as I proceeded from one chapter to the next.

Such perceived shortcomings should not detract from what is an important addition to scholarship on haiku and its role in shaping not only Beat poetics but American literature at large. As noted earlier, Hakutani's extensive knowledge of Eastern philosophies and what appears to be his lifelong study of haiku's role in shaping the trajectory of American literature makes *Jack Kerouac and the Traditions of Classic and Modern Haiku* a welcome addition to anyone's library. Lastly, for those not in possession of Kerouac's *Book of Haikus* (2003), the inclusion of a generous selection of Kerouac's haiku in part two of the book functions as an appropriate gesture in which to end this study, pointing the reader in the direction of their own journey through Kerouac's impressive work.

autumn migration
not recognizing myself
in the mirror

Poet/Artist: Dian Duchin Reed

Juxta *Contributors*

The haiku and haiga of Stephen ADDISS have appeared widely. Lately he is concentrating on ink-cuts (a form of paintilligraphy) and wood-fired teabowls. His books include *Cloud Calligraphy, A Haiku Menagerie, The Art of Zen, Haiga: Haiku-Painting, The Art of Chinese Calligraphy, Haiku People, A Haiku Garden, Haiku Humor, Tao Te Ching, Japanese Calligraphy, Haiku: An Anthology*, and *The Art of Haiku*.

THOMAS GEYER is Professor of Experimental Psychology, co-director of the international and interdisciplinary M.Sc. program in "Neuro-Cognitive Psychology". He is the head of "Cognitive Imaging" at the Department of Psychology (administrating the f/MRI research scanner) and leads the "MEMVIS" (MEMory in VIsual Search) research group at the Department of Psychology. He is deputy spokesperson of the DFG (German Research Council) funded research group "Active Perception".

DAVID GRAYSON has been writing haiku and senryu for twenty years. He authored *Discovering Fire: Haiku & Essays* (Red Moon Press, 2016), and edited *Full of Moonlight* (HSA 2016 Members' Anthology). He has been featured in *A New Resonance 6* (Red Moon Press, 2009), *My Neighbor* (Two Autumns Press, 2009) and *Spring Haiku in the Park 2018* (Yuki Teikei Society). He has edited two volumes in the Two Autumns book series. He lives in the San Francisco Bay Area with his family.

JIM KACIAN is founder and president of The Haiku Foundation (2009), founder and owner of Red Moon Press (1993), editor-in-chief of *Haiku in English: The First Hundred Years*, the definitive work on the subject (W. W. Norton, 2013), and managing editor of *Juxtapositions*. His latest book of haiku and sequences is *after / image* (Red Moon Press, 2018).

 TORU KIUCHI is former Professor of English at Nihon University, Japan. His teaching and research interests include haiku and African American literature. He is the author of *American Haiku: New Readings, Richard Wright: A Documented Chronology, 1908-1960*, with Yoshinobu Hakutani, and *The Critical Response in Japan to African American Writers*, with Robert Butler and Yoshinobu Hakutani; and a translator of *Richard Wright's Haiku: This Other World* with Michiko Watanabe.

 HEINRICH R. LIESEFELD studied psychology at Saarland University. He obtained his PhD in 2012 within the scope of the IRTG Adaptive Minds hosted by Saarland University and the Chinese Academy of Sciences (Beijing). He is now a tenure-track Researcher for Applied Statistics and Cognitive Modeling at the University of Bremen. His current research focuses on distraction and priority computations within the fields of spatial selective attention and visual working memory, using psychophysics, electroencephalography, eye tracking, and computational modelling.

 TOM MORGAN is Director of Race and Ethnic Studies and Associate Professor of English at the University of Dayton. His research focuses on the politics of narrative form, African American haiku, and the short story in late nineteenth-century periodical culture. His published work includes essays on James Weldon Johnson, Paul Laurence Dunbar, Richard Wright, Kate Chopin, and Stephen Crane, and he edited *The Complete Stories of Paul Laurence Dunbar* with Gene Andrew Jarrett. He is also moderately obsessed with metaphor.

 HERMAN J. MÜLLER is Professor (Chair) of General & Experimental Psychology at Ludwig-Maximilians-Universität, München. In 2014, he received the Wilhelm Wundt Medal, and was made an Honorary Member, of the German Psychology Society (DGPs), for his contributions to fundamental psychological science. He has co-/authored over 300 original research articles published in international journals of *Experimental Psychology* and *Cognitive Neuroscience*.

 STELLA PIERIDES British poet and writer, serves on the Board of Directors of The Haiku Foundation. Her work has been published and anthologized widely. Books include: *Of This World* (2017) and *In the Garden of Absence* (2012), both HSA Merit Book Award winners, *Feeding the Doves* (2012/13), and *Even Paranoids Have Enemies: New Perspectives on Paranoia and Persecution* (co-editor, 1998). Stella has served as managing editor of *Haikupedia*, The Haiku Foundation Encyclopedia of Haiku, and as manager of *Per Diem*, the Daily Haiku feature of the Foundation.

 CE ROSENOW is the co-author with Maurice Hamington of *Care Ethics and Poetry* and the co-editor with Bob Arnold of *The Next One Thousand Years: The Selected Poems of Cid Corman*. Her essays have appeared in various collections and journals including recent publications in *American Haiku: New Readings, African American Haiku: Cultural Visions*, and *The Journal of Ethnic American Literature*. She is the former president of the Haiku Society of America.

 TIM SHANER is the author *I Hate Fiction: A Novel* (Spuyten Duyvil, 2018) and the poetry collection *Picture X* (Airlie Press, 2014). His work has appeared in *Plumwood Mountain, Capitalism, Nature, Socialism, The Poetic Labor Project, Colorado Review, The Claudius App, Jacket, Kiosk* and elsewhere. He has an MA in Creative Writing from Antioch University (London) and a Ph.D. from SUNY-Buffalo's Poetics Program. He teaches writing at Lane Community College in Eugene, Oregon.

 QUIRIN WÜRSCHINGER is research assistant at the Chair of Modern English Linguistics at LMU Munich. He uses computational methods to study cognitive and sociolinguistic aspects of language and language use. His recent research interests include lexical innovation, social network analysis, and machine learning approaches for modelling semantic variation and change. His work is based on a variety of data sources, ranging from social media and web data to linguistic corpora and haiku.

Juxta *Staff*

The haiku and haiga of Stephen ADDISS have appeared widely. Lately he is concentrating on ink-cuts (a form of paintilligraphy) and wood-fired teabowls. His books include *Cloud Calligraphy, A Haiku Menagerie, The Art of Zen, Haiga: Haiku-Painting, The Art of Chinese Calligraphy, Haiku People, A Haiku Garden, Haiku Humor, Tao Te Ching, Japanese Calligraphy, Haiku: An Anthology,* and *The Art of Haiku.*

DAVID GRAYSON has been writing haiku and senryu for twenty years. He authored *Discovering Fire: Haiku & Essays* (Red Moon Press, 2016), and edited *Full of Moonlight* (HSA 2016 Members' Anthology). He has been featured in *A New Resonance 6* (Red Moon Press, 2009), *My Neighbor* (Two Autumns Press, 2009) and *Spring Haiku in the Park 2018* (Yuki Teikei Society). He edited of two volumes in the Two Autumns book series. He lives in the San Francisco Bay Area with his family.

JOSH HOCKENSMITH is a writer, book artist, and librarian who has worked with haiku since the 1990s when a student at the University of Richmond. He helped found the Richmond Haiku Workshop, which publllished *South by Southeast* 1999 – 2013. He is interested in book arts, the history and future of the book, and literary translation. He is the library assistant at Sloane Art Library at the University of North Carolina-Chapel Hill, where he is also working toward an MA in Art History.

JIM KACIAN is founder and president of The Haiku Foundation (2009), founder and owner of Red Moon Press (1993), editor-in-chief of *Haiku in English: The First Hundred Years,* the definitive work on the subject (W. W. Norton, 2013), and managing editor of *Juxtapositions.* His latest book of haiku and sequences is *after / image* (Red Moon Press, 2018).

 ADAM L. KERN first became interested in haiku as a high school exchange student outside of Tokyo. He studied Japanese literature at Minnesota and Harvard, where he earned a Ph.D. before joining the faculty for nearly a decade. He is author of *The Penguin Book of Haiku* (2018) and *Manga from the Floating World* (Harvard University Asia Center, 2006 and 2019). He co-edited *A Kamigata Anthology: Literature from Japan's Metropolitan Centers, 1600-1750* (Hawai'i, 2020). He is Professor of Japanese Literature and Visual Culture at the University of Wisconsin-Madison.

 SHRIKAANTH KRISHNAMURTHY is a psychiatrist from Bengaluru, India living in England. He writes in several languages. His *haikai* writings appear regularly in reputed journals and anthologies and have won prizes. Former editor of *Cattails* & *Blithe Spirit* (British Haiku Society), and former proofreader for journals *Cattails* and *Skylark*, he now edits and publishes *ephemerae*, a print journal for all things *haikai* and tanka.

 CE ROSENOW is the co-author with Maurice Hamington of *Care Ethics and Poetry* and the co-editor with Bob Arnold of *The Next One Thousand Years: The Selected Poems of Cid Corman*. Her essays have appeared in various collections and journals including recent publications in *American Haiku: New Readings, African American Haiku: Cultural Visions,* and *The Journal of Ethnic American Literature*. She is the former president of the Haiku Society of America.

 DAVE RUSSO's haiku have appeared in *Frogpond, Modern Haiku, Acorn,* and other journals. He is included in the *New Resonance 5* anthology from Red Moon Press. He organizes events for the North Carolina Haiku Society and is the web administrator for NCHS and The Haiku Foundation, and is a founding member of both.

 CRYSTAL SIMONE SMITH is the author of four poetry chapbooks including *Wildflowers: Haiku, Senryu, and Haibun* (2016). She is also a co-author of *One Windows Light: A Collection of Haiku*, Unicorn Press, (2018). Her work has appeared in numerous journals including: *Callaloo, Nimrod, Modern Haiku, Frogpond, The Heron's Nest,* and *Acorn*. She is the Founder and Managing Editor of Backbone Press.

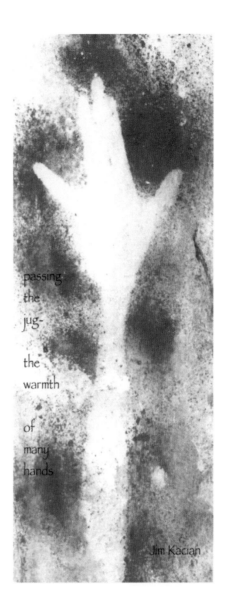

passing
the
jug-

the
warmth

of
many
hands

Jim Kacian

passing the jug the warmth of many hands

Poet: Jim Kacian
Artist: anonymous

Printed in Poland
by Amazon Fulfillment
Poland Sp. z o.o., Wrocław

67835861R00098